CW01655800

abc IAN ALLAN British Rail 1978

MOTIVE POWER

COMBINED VOLUME

ISBN 0 7110 0851 5

LONDON

IAN ALLAN LTD

CONTENTS

DIESEL SCENE

Developments on the BR diesel fleet in the past twelve months have included few noteworthy events, and in the main have been confined to consolidation of existing standard types with further applications of dual braking and withdrawal of non-standard types. The final members of the "Western" Class 52 diesel-hydraulics lasted into early 1977, and upon withdrawal four (Nos. 1010/3/23/62) passed into private ownership. Later in the year, the Class 07 diesel-electric 0-6-0s which had replaced former USA Class steam locomotives in Southampton Docks, were themselves withdrawn. With the "Westerns" gone, interest centred around the diminishing ranks of Class 24 Bo-Bos, of which a number were stored awaiting their fate; the whole class being due for extinction in early 1978.

The Silver Jubilee festivities produced two decorated Class 47s on the ER, and there was the announcement that WR Class 50s were to be given "Warship" names. Some of these names come from more illustrious vessels than those applied to the diesel-hydraulic locos. Stratford turned out a number of Class 47s with silver-painted roofs, and Class 08 shunter 08 531 appeared resplendent in its former green livery.

Deliveries of Class 56 locomotives continued throughout the year principally those built by BREL, Doncaster, and included the last arrival from Romania. The class entered traffic on some colliery-power station merry-go-round workings. The only other diesel power units to enter traffic were further power cars for HST sets and these included the first of the Class 254 vehicles for ER services. The prototype HST set 252 001 was withdrawn and transferred to BR Research for test purposes. Some members of each of classes 03, 08, 20, 24, 25, 26, 27, 40 and 44 were taken out of traffic.

British Rail diesel locomotives are listed in this publication in numerical order and under the numerical classification system introduced in 1968. Each locomotive carries a five-digit number, the first two digits of which indicate the class of locomotive (generally, the lower numbers indicate the least powerful locomotives). The remaining three digits are the individual locomotive identification; the first of these three often indicates a sub-class (thus 47 601 is Class 47/6). Such a sub-class would incorporate detail differences from the main batch. Locomotives reclassified from one section to another receive new numbers.

The headings give the main details of each class, showing manufacturer of diesel engine, power control equipment, and mechanical parts. The power rating is shown in b.h.p. and in the kW equivalent. The headings also indicate the type of train brake and heating fitted, and the original "D" prefix number series. It should be noted that some classes were modified or renumbered at random from the original number series, and in many instances the first locomotive in the class list was not originally the first locomotive. Weights of locomotives in the same class may vary due to differing braking or heating equipment.

Diesel and electric locomotive wheel arrangements are described by a development of the continental system. This calculates by axles and uses letters to denote driving axles and numerals to denote non-powered carrying axles. A locomotive with two bogies each having two powered axles is a B-B (three axles—C-C, etc.). If the axles on a bogie or frame are individually powered, such as in a diesel-electric by one traction motor per axle, the suffix letter "o" is added. Thus the Class 55 is a Co-Co, and the former Class 52 a C-C. Shunting locomotives with a rigid frame and coupled wheels follow steam locomotive pattern and are known by the Whyte system as 0-4-0, 0-6-0, etc.

The information shown in each class heading follows a style similar to that used on the standard information panel applied to BR locomotives. The layout of this panel is shown below:

AB/VB Class:
Weight tons:
Brake force tons:
RA:
ETH Index:
Max. speed m.p.h.:

The code AB/VB indicates air or vacuum train braking, although on classes where all locomotives are dual braked, this may be omitted. Class, weight (always in working order) and maximum speed are all self-explanatory. The brake force is an indication of the locomotive's stopping power. It is shown in tons and calculated by a formula dependent on weight and certain other factors. All BR routes have a classification code which indicates their ability to carry concentrated weight (the lower the number, the lighter the weight). The RA (route availability) number is based on the weight per axle of the locomotive, and no locomotive may work over a route with a lower RA number than itself. Locomotives fitted with electric train heating equipment will also show an ETH index on this panel. Each coach has an ETH rating, and the total of all the coach ratings in a train must not exceed the ETH index figure on the locomotive. Original names of locomotives are shown where appropriate, although nameplates may have been removed subsequently.

The numbers of locomotives in service have been checked to the following dates: LMR 27 November, ER 27 November, SR 17 October, WR 26 November, SCR 26 November. See also "Late Information" section.

Information in this booklet has been checked against BR TOPS Records.

This booklet shows the latest known stock position at the time of going to press. To allow readers to keep their records up to date, motive-power changes (new building, withdrawals, reallocations, reclassifications, renumberings, etc.) are published every month in the Ian Allan magazines *Railway World* and *Modern Railways*. Notification of any errors found in the booklet should be sent to The Editors, BR Locomotives, Ian Allan Ltd. The publishers cannot enter into correspondence about individual locomotive types or about more general railway topics.

N.B. British Rail High Speed Train power cars are listed individually in this publication, and by unit numbers in the *ABC Diesel Multiple Units*.

COUPLING OF DIESEL LOCOMOTIVES

Main-line diesel locomotives of most classes are equipped to operate in multiple with locomotives having similar control systems. In order to distinguish locomotives which can operate in this way, a colour code symbol is painted above each buffer and repeated in miniature on the plug and socket covers.

Type of Locomotive	*Coupling symbol*
All diesel-electric locomotives with electro-pneumatic control.	★ BLUE STAR
All diesel-electric locomotives with electro-magnetic control.	● RED CIRCLE
Class 50 diesel-electric locomotives	■ ORANGE SQUARE
Class 17 diesel-electric locomotives	♦ RED DIAMOND

Cover: *A Class 87 25 kV a.c. electric locomotive leaves Shugborough Tunnel on an express.* M. G. G. Rickard

Back Cover: *Class 253 HST No 253 024 approaches Reading.* Anthony Wirkus

SAFETY FIRST

In 1976 no passengers were killed travelling on British Railways—demonstrating that properly used railways are very safe.

Inevitably each year a number of people are killed whilst playing or trespassing on the lines—sadly, even experienced and trained railway staff become involved in mishaps, demonstrating the inherent dangers even for those whose duties take them to the wrong side of the fence.

British Rail welcomes the interest in its operations shown by railway enthusiasts using this book. But railway lines, maintenance depots, sidings and sheds are dangerous places unless your visit is by invitation and properly supervised.

Otherwise your presence there is probably illegal, certainly not welcome and could be FATAL.

British Railways Board

Class 01 0-4-0

Diesel mechanical shunter built 1956
Engine: Gardner 6L3 of 153 b.h.p. (114 kW)
Mechanical parts: Barclay
Weight: 25 tons
Brake force: 16 tons. No train brake
Maximum tractive effort: 12,750 lb
Transmission: Mechanical. Vulcan-Sinclair rigid type hydraulic coupling. Wilson S.E. 4 type four-speed epicyclic gearbox. Wiseman type 15 RLGB reverse and final drive unit
Route availability: 1
Maximum speed: 14 m.p.h.
No train heating
Previous no. series: D2953–2954

01 001	01 002

TOTAL: 2

Class 03 0-6-0

Diesel mechanical shunter built 1957–61
Engine: Gardner 8L3 of 204 b.h.p. (152 kW)
Mechanical parts: BR
Weight: 30–31 tons
Brake force: 13 tons. Vacuum braked (¶ dual braked)
Maximum tractive effort: 15,300 lb
Transmission: Mechanical. Vulcan-Sinclair type 23 fluid coupling. Wilson-Drewry C.A.5 type five-speed epicyclic gearbox. Type RF 11 spiral bevel reverse and final drive unit
Route availability: 1
Maximum speed: 28 m.p.h.
No train heating
Previous no. series: D2000–2199

03 008	03 017	03 022
03 016	03 021	03 026
03 029	03 081	03 154
03 034	03 084¶	03 158¶
03 045	03 086¶	03 160
03 047	03 089¶	03 161
03 050	03 094¶	03 162¶
03 056	03 103	03 168
03 059¶	03 107	03 170¶
03 060	03 111	03 175
03 061	03 112¶	03 179¶
03 062	03 119	03 180¶
03 063¶	03 120	03 189
03 064	03 121	03 196¶
03 066¶	03 129	03 197¶
03 067	03 141	03 370
03 069	03 142	03 371¶
03 072	03 144	03 382
03 073¶	03 145	03 389
03 078¶	03 149	03 397¶
03 079	03 151	03 399¶
03 080	03 152¶	

Nos. 03 119/30/41/2/4/5/51/2 have cut-down cab for working on the BPGV line

TOTAL: 64

Class 05 0-6-0

Diesel mechanical shunter built 1955
Engine: Gardner 8L3 of 204 b.h.p. (152 kW)
Mechanical parts: Hunslet
Weight: 32 tons
Brake force: 21·5 tons. Vacuum brake
Maximum tractive effort: 14,500 lb
Transmission: Mechanical. Hunslet patent friction clutch. Hunslet four-speed gearbox incorporating reverse and final drive gears
Route availability: 2
Maximum speed: 18 m.p.h.
No train heating
Previous no. series: D2550–2618

05 001

TOTAL: 1

Class 06 0-4-0

Diesel mechanical shunter built 1958–60
Engine: Gardner 8L3 of 204 b.h.p. (152 kW)
Mechanical parts: Barclay
Weight: 37 tons
Brake force: 25 tons. Vacuum brake
Maximum tractive effort: 19,800 lb
Transmission: Mechanical Vulcan-Sinclair type 23 fluid coupling. Wilson-Drewry C.A.5 type five-speed epicyclic gearbox. Wiseman type 15 RLGB reverse and final drive unit
Route availability: 5
Maximum speed: 23 m.p.h.
No train heating
Previous no. series: D2410–2444

06 002	06 004	06 006
06 003	06 005	06 008

TOTAL: 6

Class 08 0-6-0

Built 1952–62 to standard design adopted for 350 h.p. shunter
Engine: English Electric 6-cyl. 6KT of 350 b.h.p. (261 kW)
Mechanical parts: BR
Weight: 49–50 tons
Brake force: 33 tons. Vacuum brake (¶ dual braked) (● air braked)
Maximum tractive effort: 35,000 lb
Power/control equipment: English Electric. Two EE 506 traction motors. Double reduction gear drive
Route availability: 5
Maximum speed: 15/20 m.p.h.
No train heating
Previous no. series: D3000–3116, D3127–3136, D3167–3438, D3454–3472, D3503–3611, D3652–4048

08 001	08 064	08 125
08 003	08 067	08 126
08 004	08 068	08 127
08 005	08 069	08 128
08 006	08 070	08 129
08 008	08 071	08 130
08 010	08 075	08 131
08 011	08 076	08 132
08 014	08 078	08 133
08 015	08 079	08 134
08 016	08 080	08 136
08 018	08 081	08 137
08 019	08 082	08 138
08 021	08 083	08 139
08 022	08 084	08 141
08 023	08 085	08 142
08 024	08 086	08 144
08 025	08 087	08 145
08 026	08 088	08 146
08 027	08 089	08 147
08 028	08 091	08 148
08 029	08 092	08 149
08 030	08 093	08 150
08 031	08 094	08 151
08 033	08 095	08 152
08 035	08 096	08 153
08 036	08 097	08 154
08 037	08 098	08 155
08 041	08 099	08 156
08 042	08 100	08 158
08 043	08 101	08 159
08 044	08 102	08 160
08 045	08 103	08 161
08 046	08 104	08 162
08 047	08 105	08 163
08 048	08 106	08 164
08 049	08 107	08 165
08 050	08 108	08 166
08 051	08 109	08 168
08 052	08 110	08 169
08 053	08 112	08 170
08 054	08 113	08 171
08 055	08 114	08 172
08 056	08 115	08 173
08 058	08 116	08 174
08 059	08 118	08 175
08 060	08 120	08 176
08 061	08 121	08 177
08 062	08 123	08 178
08 063	08 124	08 180

Class 03 0-6-0 shunter No. 03 370 [*B. J. Nicolle*

Class 06 0-4-0 shunter No. 06 004 [*N. E. Preedy*

Class 08 0-6-0 shunter No. 08 863 *[B. J. Nicolle*

08 181
08 182
08 183
08 184
08 185
08 186
08 187
08 188
08 189
08 190
08 191
08 192
08 193
08 194
08 195
08 196
08 197
08 198
08 199
08 200
08 201
08 202
08 203
08 204
08 205
08 206
08 207
08 208
08 209
08 210
08 211
08 212
08 213
08 214
08 215
08 216
08 217
08 218
08 219
08 220
08 221
08 222
08 223
08 224
08 225
08 226
08 227
08 228
08 229
08 230
08 231
08 232
08 233
08 234
08 235
08 237
08 238
08 239
08 240
08 241
08 242
08 243●
08 244
08 245
08 246
08 247
08 248
08 249
08 250
08 251
08 252
08 253
08 254
08 255
08 256
08 257
08 258
08 259
08 260
08 261
08 262
08 263
08 264
08 265
08 266
08 267
08 268
08 269
08 270
08 271
08 272
08 273
08 274
08 275
08 277
08 279
08 280
08 281
08 282
08 283
08 284
08 285
08 286
08 287
08 288
08 289
08 290
08 291
08 292
08 293
08 294
08 295
08 296
08 297
08 298
08 299
08 300
08 301
08 302
08 303
08 304
08 305
08 306
08 307
08 308
08 309
08 311
08 312
08 313
08 314
08 315
08 317
08 319
08 320
08 321
08 322
08 323
08 324
08 325
08 326
08 327
08 328
08 329
08 330
08 331
08 332
08 333
08 334
08 335
08 336
08 337
08 338
08 339
08 340
08 341
08 342
08 343
08 344
08 345
08 346
08 347
08 348
08 349
08 350
08 351
08 352
08 353
08 354
08 355
08 356
08 359
08 360
08 361
08 362
08 363
08 364
08 365
08 366
08 367
08 368
08 369
08 370
08 371
08 372
08 373
08 374
08 375
08 376
08 377
08 378
08 379
08 380
08 381
08 382
08 383
08 384
08 385
08 386
08 387
08 388
08 389
08 390
08 391
08 392
08 393
08 394
08 395
08 396
08 397
08 398
08 399
08 400
08 401
08 402
08 403
08 404
08 405
08 406
08 407
08 408
08 409
08 410
08 411
08 412
08 413
08 414●
08 415
08 416
08 417
08 418
08 419
08 420
08 421
08 422
08 423
08 424
08 425
08 427
08 428●
08 429
08 430
08 431
08 432
08 433
08 434
08 435
08 436
08 437
08 438
08 439
08 440
08 441●
08 442●
08 443
08 444
08 445●
08 446
08 447
08 448
08 449
08 450
08 451
08 452
08 453
08 454
08 455
08 456
08 457
08 458
08 459
08 460●
08 461
08 462
08 463
08 464
08 465
08 466
08 467
08 468
08 469
08 470
08 471
08 472
08 473
08 474
08 475
08 476
08 477
08 478
08 479
08 480●
08 481
08 482
08 483●
08 484●
08 485
08 486
08 487
08 488
08 489●

08 490
08 491
08 492
08 493●
08 494
08 495
08 496
08 497
08 498
08 499
08 500
08 501
08 502
08 503
08 504
08 505
08 506
08 507●
08 508
08 509
08 510●
08 511
08 512●
08 513
08 514●
08 515
08 516
08 517●
08 518●
08 519
08 520
08 521●
08 522
08 523
08 524
08 525¶
08 526¶
08 527¶
08 528¶
08 529¶
08 530¶
08 531¶
08 532¶
08 533¶
08 534¶
08 535¶
08 536¶
08 537¶
08 538¶
08 539¶
08 540¶
08 541¶
08 542¶
08 543¶
08 544¶
08 545
08 546
08 547
08 548
08 549
08 550
08 551
08 552
08 553
08 554
08 555
08 556
08 557
08 558
08 559
08 560
08 561
08 562
08 563
08 564
08 565
08 567
08 568
08 569
08 570
08 571
08 572
08 573
08 574
08 575
08 576
08 577
08 578
08 579
08 580
08 581
08 582
08 583
08 584
08 585
08 586
08 587
08 588
08 589
08 590
08 591
08 592
08 593
08 594
08 595
08 597
08 598
08 599
08 600●
08 601
08 602
08 603
08 604
08 605
08 606
08 607
08 608
08 609
08 610
08 611
08 612
08 613
08 614
08 615
08 616
08 617
08 618
08 619
08 620
08 621●
08 622
08 623
08 624
08 625
08 626
08 627●
08 628
08 629
08 630
08 631
08 632
08 633
08 634
08 635
08 636
08 637
08 638
08 639
08 640¶
08 641¶
08 642¶
08 643¶
08 644¶
08 645¶
08 646¶
08 647¶
08 648¶
08 649¶
08 650¶
08 651¶
08 652¶
08 653¶
08 654¶
08 655¶
08 656
08 657
08 658
08 659
08 660
08 661
08 662
08 663
08 664
08 665
08 666
08 667
08 668
08 669
08 670
08 671
08 672
08 673
08 674
08 675
08 676
08 677
08 678●
08 680
08 681
08 682
08 683
08 684
08 685
08 686
08 687
08 688●
08 689
08 690
08 691
08 692
08 693
08 694
08 695
08 696
08 697
08 698
08 699
08 700●
08 701
08 702
08 703●
08 704
08 705
08 706
08 707
08 708
08 709
08 710
08 711
08 712
08 713
08 714
08 715
08 716
08 717
08 718
08 719
08 720
08 721
08 722
08 723
08 724
08 725
08 726
08 727
08 728
08 729
08 730
08 731
08 732
08 733
08 734
08 735
08 736
08 737¶
08 738¶
08 739¶
08 740¶
08 741¶
08 742¶
08 743¶
08 744¶
08 745¶
08 746¶
08 747¶
08 748¶
08 749¶
08 750¶
08 751¶
08 752¶
08 753¶
08 754¶
08 755¶
08 756¶
08 757¶
08 758¶
08 759¶
08 760¶
08 761¶
08 762¶
08 763¶
08 764¶
08 765¶
08 766¶
08 767¶
08 768¶
08 769
08 770
08 771
08 772
08 773
08 774
08 775
08 776
08 777
08 778
08 779
08 780
08 781
08 782
08 783
08 784
08 785
08 786
08 787
08 788
08 789
08 790
08 791
08 792

Class 09 0-6-0 shunter No. 09 024 [*B. J. Nicolle*

Class 13 0-6-0+0-6-0 hump shunter No. 13 001 [*K. Lane*

08 793	08 843¶	08 893¶
08 794	08 844¶	08 894¶
08 795	08 845¶	08 895¶
08 796	08 846¶	08 896¶
08 797	08 847¶	08 897¶
08 798	08 848¶	08 898¶
08 799	08 849¶	08 899¶
08 800	08 850¶	08 900¶
08 801	08 851¶	08 901¶
08 802	08 852¶	08 902¶
08 803	08 853¶	08 903¶
08 804	08 854¶	08 904¶
08 805	08 855¶	08 905¶
08 806●	08 856¶	08 906¶
08 807	08 857¶	08 907¶
08 808	08 858¶	08 908¶
08 809	08 859¶	08 909¶
08 810	08 860	08 910¶
08 811●	08 861	08 911¶
08 812	08 862	08 912¶
08 813	08 863	08 913¶
08 814●	08 864	08 914¶
08 815	08 865	08 915¶
08 816●	08 866	08 916¶
08 817	08 867	08 917¶
08 818	08 868	08 918¶
08 819	08 869	08 919¶
08 820	08 870	08 920¶
08 821	08 871	08 921¶
08 822	08 872¶	08 922¶
08 823●	08 873¶	08 923¶
08 824●	08 874¶	08 924¶
08 825●	08 875¶	08 925¶
08 826	08 876¶	08 926¶
08 827	08 877¶	08 927¶
08 828	08 878¶	08 928¶
08 829●	08 879¶	08 929¶
08 830¶	08 880¶	08 930¶
08 831¶	08 881¶	08 931¶
08 832¶	08 882¶	08 932¶
08 833¶	08 883¶	08 933¶
08 834¶	08 884¶	08 934¶
08 835¶	08 885¶	08 935¶
08 836¶	08 886¶	08 936¶
08 837¶	08 887¶	08 937¶
08 838¶	08 888¶	08 938¶
08 839¶	08 889¶	08 939¶
08 840¶	08 890¶	08 940¶
08 841¶	08 891¶	08 941¶
08 842¶	08 892¶	08 942¶

08 943¶	08 949¶	08 954¶
08 944¶	08 950¶	08 955¶
08 945¶	08 951¶	08 956¶
08 946¶	08 952¶	08 957¶
08 947¶	08 953¶	08 958¶
08 948¶		

TOTAL: 916

Class 09 0-6-0

Uprated version of 08, built 1959–62
Engine: English Electric 6-cyl. 6KT of 400 b.h.p. (298 kW)
Mechanical parts: BR
Weight: 50 tons
Brake force: 33 tons. Dual braked
Maximum tractive effort: 25,000 lb
Power/control equipment: English Electric. Two EE 506 traction motors. Double reduction gear drive
Route availability: 5
Maximum speed: 27 m.p.h.
No train heating
Previous no. series: D3665–3771, D3719–3721, D4099–4114

09 001	09 010	09 019
09 002	09 011	09 020
09 003	09 012	09 021
09 004	09 013	09 022
09 005	09 014	09 023
09 006	09 015	09 024
09 007	09 016	09 025
09 008	09 017	09 026
09 009	09 018	

TOTAL: 26

Class 13 — 0-6-0+0-6-0

Permanently coupled "master" and "slave" units, converted in 1965 from Class 08 0-6-0 diesels for hump shunting in Tinsley Yard. The cab of the "slave" unit has been removed and both units are specially weighted
Engine: Two English Electric 6-cyl. 6KT. Total 800 b.h.p. (597 kW)
Mechanical parts: BR
Weight: 120 tons
Brake force: 66 tons. Vacuum brake
Maximum tractive effort: 70,000 lb
Power/control equipment: English Electric. Four EE 506 traction motors. Double reduction gear drive
Route availability: 8
Maximum speed: 20 m.p.h.
No train heating
Previous no. series: D4500–4502

13 001	13 002	13 003

TOTAL: 3

Class 20 — Bo-Bo★

Single cab design built 1957–67. Adopted as standard 1000 b.h.p. design
Engine: English Electric 8 SVT Mk. 2 of 1,000 b.h.p. (746 kW)
Mechanical parts: English Electric
Weight: 72–3 tons
Brake force: 61 tons. Vacuum brake (¶ dual braked)
Maximum tractive effort: 42,000 lb
Power/control equipment: English Electric. Four EE 526/5D or 526/8D traction motors
Route availability: 5
Maximum speed: 75 m.p.h.
No train heating
Previous no. series: D8000–8199, D8300–8327

20 001	20 057	20 110
20 002¶	20 058	20 111¶
20 003	20 059	20 112
20 004	20 060	20 113
20 005	20 061	20 114¶
20 006	20 063	20 115¶
20 007	20 064¶	20 116¶
20 008	20 065	20 117
20 009¶	20 066¶	20 118¶
20 010	20 067	20 119
20 011¶	20 068	20 120
20 013	20 069	20 121
20 015¶	20 070	20 122¶
20 016	20 071	20 123¶
20 017	20 072	20 124¶
20 019	20 073	20 125¶
20 020	20 075	20 126
20 021	20 076¶	20 127
20 022	20 077	20 128
20 023	20 078	20 129
20 025	20 080	20 130
20 026	20 081	20 131
20 027	20 082	20 132
20 028	20 083¶	20 133
20 029	20 084	20 134
20 030	20 085¶	20 135
20 031	20 086¶	20 136
20 032	20 087	20 137¶
20 034	20 088	20 138¶
20 035¶	20 089¶	20 139
20 036¶	20 090	20 140
20 037	20 091	20 141
20 039¶	20 092	20 142¶
20 040	20 093	20 143
20 041	20 094	20 144¶
20 042	20 095	20 145¶
20 043	20 096	20 146¶
20 044	20 097	20 147
20 045	20 098	20 148
20 046	20 099	20 149¶
20 047	20 100	20 150¶
20 048	20 101	20 151
20 049	20 102	20 152¶
20 050	20 103	20 153¶
20 051	20 104	20 154¶
20 052	20 105	20 155¶
20 053	20 106	20 156¶
20 054	20 107	20 157
20 055	20 108	20 158
20 056	20 109	20 159

Class 20 Bo-Bo No. 20 140 [N. E. Preedy

20 160	20 183	20 206¶
20 161	20 184¶	20 207¶
20 162¶	20 185	20 208
20 163	20 186	20 209
20 164¶	20 187	20 210
20 165¶	20 188	20 211
20 166	20 189	20 212
20 167¶	20 190	20 213
20 168	20 191¶	20 214
20 169	20 192	20 215
20 170	20 193	20 216¶
20 171	20 194	20 217¶
20 172	20 195	20 218¶
20 173	20 196	20 219¶
20 174¶	20 197	20 220¶
20 175¶	20 198	20 221¶
20 176	20 199	20 222¶
20 177	20 200¶	20 223¶
20 178	20 201¶	20 224¶
20 179¶	20 202¶	20 225¶
20 180	20 203¶	20 226¶
20 181	20 204¶	20 227¶
20 182	20 205¶	20 228

TOTAL: 219

Class 24 Bo-Bo★

BR design introduced 1958
Engine: Sulzer 6-cyl. 6LDA28 of 1,160 b.h.p. (865 kW)
Mechanical parts: BR
Weight: 77–79 tons
Brake force: 64 tons. Vacuum brake
Maximum tractive effort: 40,000 lb
Power/control equipment: BTH. Four BTH 137 BY traction motors
Route availability: 6
Maximum speed: 75 m.p.h.
Steam heating (not in use)
Previous no. series: D5000–5093

Class 24/0

24 023	24 035	24 047

Class 24/1 Bo-Bo★

Development of Class 24 with reduced weight.
Details as above
Weight: 73 tons
Route availability: 5
Train heating not fitted or not in use
Previous no. series: D5094–5150

24 057	24 081	24 087
24 063	24 082	24 133

Class 24 scheduled for early withdrawal

TOTAL: 9

Class 25 Bo-Bo★

1961 development of Class 24 design with higher power, and styling changes
Engine: Sulzer 6-cyl. 6LDA 28-B of 1,250 b.h.p. (933 kW)
Mechanical parts: BR
Weight: 74 tons
Brake force: 64 tons. Vacuum brake (¶ dual braked)
Maximum tractive effort: 39,000 lb
Power/control equipment: AEI. Four AEI 137 BX traction motors
Route availability: 5
Maximum speed: 90 m.p.h.
No train heating
Previous no. series: D5151–5175

Class 25/0

25 001	25 008	25 019
25 002	25 009	25 021
25 005	25 010	25 023
25 006	25 011	25 025
25 007	25 013	

Class 25/1 Bo-Bo★

As class 25/0 with detail modifications
Power/control equipment: GEC series 1. Four AEI 253 AY traction motors

Weight: 71–5 tons
Maximum tractive effort:
45,000 lb
Steam heating, except 25 031/2
Previous no. series: D5176–5237

25 026	25 047	25 065
25 027	25 048¶	25 066
25 028	25 049	25 067
25 031	25 050	25 068
25 032¶	25 051¶	25 069
25 033	25 052§	25 070
25 034	25 053¶	25 071
25 035	25 054¶	25 072
25 036¶	25 055	25 073
25 037	25 056	25 074
25 038	25 057¶	25 075
25 039	25 058¶	25 076
25 040	25 059¶	25 077¶
25 041	25 060¶	25 078
25 042	25 061	25 079¶
25 043	25 062	25 080
25 044¶	25 063	25 081
25 046	25 064	25 082¶

TOTAL: 54

Class 25/2 **Bo-Bo★**
Further detail differences
Power/control equipment: GEC series 2. Four AEI 253 AY traction motors
Weight: 71–6 tons
25 083–7 fitted with steam heating
Previous no. series: D5233–5299, D7500–7597

25 083	25 098	25 113¶
25 084	25 099¶	25 114
25 085	25 100	25 115
25 086	25 101	25 116
25 087	25 102	25 117¶
25 088¶	25 103	25 118
25 089¶	25 104	25 119
25 090	25 105	25 120¶
25 091	25 106¶	25 121
25 092	25 107	25 122
25 093	25 108	25 123
25 094	25 109¶	25 124
25 095¶	25 110	25 125
25 096	25 111	25 126
25 097¶	25 112	25 127

25 129	25 169	25 209
25 130	25 170	25 210
25 131	25 171	25 211
25 132	25 172	25 212
25 133	25 173	25 213
25 134	25 175¶	25 214
25 135	25 176	25 215
25 136	25 177	25 216
25 137	25 178¶	25 217
25 138	25 179	25 218¶
25 139	25 180	25 219
25 140	25 181	25 220
25 141	25 182	25 221¶
25 142	25 183¶	25 222¶
25 143	25 184¶	25 223
25 144	25 185	25 224
25 145¶	25 186	25 225
25 146	25 187	25 226¶
25 147	25 188	25 227
25 148	25 189	25 228¶
25 149	25 190	25 229¶
25 150	25 191	25 230¶
25 151	25 192	25 231¶
25 152	25 193	25 232¶
25 153	25 194¶	25 233¶
25 154	25 195	25 234¶
25 155	25 196¶	25 235
25 156	25 197¶	25 236¶
25 157	25 198¶	25 237¶
25 158	25 199¶	25 238
25 159	25 200¶	25 239¶
25 160	25 201¶	25 240¶
25 161	25 202¶	25 241¶
25 162	25 203¶	25 242¶
25 163	25 204¶	25 243¶
25 164	25 205¶	25 244
25 165	25 206¶	25 245¶
25 166	25 207¶	25 246¶
25 167	25 208	25 247¶
25 168		

TOTAL: 162

Class 25/3 **Bo-Bo★**
Final development of Class 25 without end gangway connections
Power/control equipment: GEC Series 3. Four AEI 253 AY traction motors
Weight: 71 tons

Class 24 Bo-Bo No. 24 091 [*N. E. Preedy*

Class 25 Bo-Bo No. 25 058 [*B. J. Nicolle*

Class 25 Bo-Bos Nos. 25 143 and 25 173 at Caersws [J. Scrace

Mechanical parts: Beyer Peacock/BR
No train heating
Previous no. series: D7598–7677

25 248	25 276¶	25 303¶
25 249¶	25 277¶	25 304
25 250¶	25 278¶	25 305¶
25 251¶	25 279¶	25 306
25 252	25 280	25 307¶
25 253	25 281	25 308¶
25 254¶	25 282¶	25 309¶
25 256¶	25 283¶	25 310¶
25 257¶	25 284¶	25 311¶
25 258¶	25 285¶	25 312¶
25 259¶	25 286¶	25 313¶
25 260	25 287¶	25 314¶
25 261	25 288¶	25 315¶
25 262¶	25 289¶	25 316¶
25 263	25 290	25 317¶
25 264	25 291	25 318¶
25 265¶	25 292	25 319¶
25 266¶	25 293	25 320
25 267	25 294	25 321
25 268¶	25 295¶	25 322¶
25 269¶	25 296¶	25 323
25 270	25 297¶	25 324¶
25 271	25 298¶	25 325
25 272	25 299	25 326¶
25 273	25 300¶	25 327¶
25 274	25 301¶	
25 275	25 302	

TOTAL: 79

Class 26 Bo-Bo★

Introduced 1958 as design alternative to Class 24
Engine: Sulzer 6-cyl. 6LDA28 of 1,160 b.h.p. (865 kW)
Mechanical parts: Birmingham RC & W
Weight: 73–79 tons
Brake force: 58 tons. Vacuum brake (26 001–7 dual braked)
Maximum tractive effort: 42,000 lb
Power/control equipment: Crompton Parkinson. Four CP C171 traction motors
Route availability: 6
Maximum speed: 80 m.p.h. (nos. 26 001–7 75 m.p.h.)
26 008–20 fitted steam heating
Previous no. series: D5300–5319

Class 26/0

26 001	26 007	26 013
26 002	26 008	26 014
26 003	26 010	26 015
26 004	26 011	26 018
26 005	26 012	26 019
26 006		

TOTAL: 17

Class 26/1 Bo-Bo★

As class 26/0 but all fitted with vacuum brake and steam heating
Power/control equipment: Crompton Parkinson. Four CP C171 D3 traction motors
Weight: 73 tons
Route availability: 5
Previous no. series: D5320–5346

26 021	26 030	26 039
26 022	26 031	26 040
26 023	26 032	26 041
26 024	26 033	26 042
26 025	26 034	26 043
26 026	26 035	26 044
26 027	26 036	26 045
26 028	26 037	26 046
26 029	26 038	

TOTAL: 26

Class 27 Bo-Bo★

1961 development of Class 26
Engine: Sulzer 6-cyl. 6LDA28-B of 1,250 b.h.p. (933 kW)
Mechanical parts: Birmingham RC & W
Weight: 71–6 tons
Brake force: 58 tons. Vacuum brake (¶dual braked)
Maximum tractive effort: 40,000 lb

Class 26 Bo-Bo No. 26 028 [*N. E. Preedy*

Power/control equipment: GEC. Four GEC WT 459 traction motors
Route availability: 5
Maximum speed: 90 m.p.h.
Steam heating, except 27 024–31
Previous no. series: Random from D5347–5415

Class 27/0

27 001	27 017	27 030
27 002	27 018	27 031
27 003	27 019	27 032
27 004	27 020	27 033
27 005	27 021	27 034
27 007	27 022	27 036
27 008	27 023	27 037
27 009	27 024	27 038¶
27 010	27 025	27 040
27 011	27 026	27 041¶
27 012	27 027	27 042
27 014	27 028	27 043
27 016	27 029	27 044

TOTAL: 43

Class 27/1 **Bo-Bo★**
As Class 27/0
Weight: 76 tons
Dual braked
Steam heating
Previous no. series: Random from D5374–5413

Fitted for push-pull working

27 101¶ 27 102¶
27 103¶ (27 118)

27 104¶	27 107¶	27 110¶
27 105¶	27 108¶	27 111¶
27 106¶	27 109¶	27 112¶

TOTAL: 12

Class 27/2 **Bo-Bo★**
As Class 27/1 but without steam heating
Dual braked
Electric train heating
Previous no. series: Random from D5384–5412

27 201¶ (27 119)
27 202¶ (27 120)
27 203¶ (27 121)
27 204¶ (27 122)
27 205¶ (27 123)
27 206¶ (27 124)
27 207¶ (27 113)
27 208¶ (27 114)
27 209¶ (27 115)
27 210¶
27 211¶ (27 117)
27 212¶ (27 103)

TOTAL: 12

Class 31 **AIA-AIA ●**
Built 1957–62. Prototype now at NRM, York
Engine: English Electric 12-cyl. 12SV of 1,470 b.h.p. (1,097 kW)
Mechanical parts: Brush
Weight: 109 tons
Brake force: 85 tons. Vacuum brake
Maximum tractive effort: 42,800 lb
Power/control equipment: Brush. Four TM 73–68 traction motors
Route availability: 5
Maximum speed: ‡80 m.p.h., 90 m.p.h.
Steam heating
Previous no. series: D5500–5519

Class 31/0: Fitted with electro-magnetic control equipment

31 002‡	31 006‡	31 015‡
31 003‡	31 008‡	31 017‡
31 004‡	31 013‡	31 019‡
31 005‡		

Scheduled for withdrawal by 31 December 1978

TOTAL: 10

Class 31/1 **AIA-AIA★**
Development of 31/0
Weight: 107–11 tons
Vacuum brake (¶dual braked)

Previous no. series:
Random from D5518–5862

31 101‡	31 152¶	31 203¶
31 102‡	31 153¶	31 204
31 103‡	31 154¶	31 205¶
31 105‡¶	31 155¶	31 206¶
31 106‡¶	31 156¶	31 207
31 107‡¶	31 158¶	31 208¶
31 108‡	31 159¶	31 209¶
31 109‡¶	31 160	31 210¶
31 110‡¶	31 161¶	31 211
31 111‡	31 162¶	31 212¶
31 112¶	31 163¶	31 213¶
31 113‡¶	31 164	31 214
31 114‡	31 165¶	31 215
31 115‡	31 166¶	31 216
31 116‡¶	31 167	31 217¶
31 117¶	31 168¶	31 218¶
31 118¶	31 169	31 219¶
31 119¶	31 170¶	31 220¶
31 120	31 171¶	31 221¶
31 121¶	31 173¶	31 222¶
31 122	31 174¶	31 223¶
31 123¶	31 175¶	31 224¶
31 124	31 176¶	31 225¶
31 125	31 177	31 226¶
31 126	31 178¶	31 227¶
31 127¶	31 179	31 228
31 128¶	31 180¶	31 229
31 129	31 181¶	31 230¶
31 130¶	31 182	31 231¶
31 131¶	31 183	31 232¶
31 132	31 184¶	31 233¶
31 133	31 185¶	31 234
31 134	31 186¶	31 235¶
31 135¶	31 187¶	31 236
31 136	31 188¶	31 237
31 137	31 189¶	31 238¶
31 138¶	31 190¶	31 239
31 139	31 191¶	31 240
31 141¶	31 192¶	31 241¶
31 142¶	31 193	31 242¶
31 143¶	31 194	31 243¶
31 144¶	31 195¶	31 244
31 145¶	31 196¶	31 245¶
31 146	31 198¶	31 246
31 147¶	31 199¶	31 247¶
31 148	31 200	31 248
31 149¶	31 201¶	31 249¶
31 151	31 202¶	31 250¶

31 251	31 277	31 302¶
31 252¶	31 278¶	31 303
31 253	31 279	31 304¶
31 254	31 280	31 305
31 255¶	31 281¶	31 306
31 256¶	31 282¶	31 307¶
31 257¶	31 283¶	31 308
31 258¶	31 284¶	31 309
31 259¶	31 285¶	31 311¶
31 260	31 286¶	31 312
31 261	31 287	31 313
31 262	31 288	31 314¶
31 263¶	31 289	31 315
31 264	31 290	31 316
31 265	31 291	31 317
31 266	31 292¶	31 318
31 268¶	31 293	31 319
31 269	31 294¶	31 320¶
31 270	31 295	31 321
31 271	31 296¶	31 322¶
31 272¶	31 297	31 323¶
31 273¶	31 298	31 324
31 274	31 299	31 325
31 275	31 300	31 326
31 276¶	31 301¶	31 327¶

TOTAL: 219

Class 31/4 **AIA-AIA★**
Development of 31/1
Weight: 108–12 tons
Steam and electric train heating (31 424 ETH only)
Dual braked.
Previous no. series:
Random from D5522–5856

31 401¶	31 414¶
31 402¶	31 415¶
31 403¶	31 416¶
31 404¶	31 417¶
31 405¶	31 418‡¶
31 406¶	31 419¶
31 407¶	31 420¶ (31 172)
31 408¶	31 421¶ (31 140)
31 409¶	31 422¶ (31 310)
31 410¶	31 423¶ (31 197)
31 411¶	31 424¶ (31 157)
31 412¶	
31 413¶	

TOTAL: 24

Class 27/1 Bo-Bo No. 27 103 [*N. E. Preedy*

Class 31/1 Bo-Bo No. 31 207 [*B. J. Nicolle*

Class 31/4 Bo-Bo No. 31 411 [*B. J. Nicolle*

Class 33 Bo-Bo★

Built 1960–2 for Southern Region
Engine: Sulzer 8-cyl. 8LDA28 pressure-charged of 1,550 b.h.p. (1,156 kW)
Mechanical parts: Birmingham RC & W
Weight: 77 tons
Brake force: 59 tons. Dual braked
Maximum tractive effort: 45,000 lb
Power/control equipment: Crompton Parkinson. Four CP C171 C2 traction motors
Route availability: 6
Maximum speed: 85 m.p.h.
Fitted with electric train-heating equipment only
Previous no. series: Random from D6500–6585

Class 33/0

33 001	33 023	33 045
33 002	33 024	33 046
33 003	33 025	33 047
33 004	33 026	33 048
33 005	33 027	33 049
33 006	33 028	33 050
33 007	33 029	33 051
33 008	33 030	33 052
33 009	33 031	33 053
33 010	33 032	33 054
33 011	33 033	33 055
33 012	33 034	33 056
33 013	33 035	33 057
33 014	33 036	33 058
33 015	33 037	33 059
33 016	33 038	33 060
33 017	33 039	33 061
33 018	33 040	33 062
33 019	33 042	33 063
33 020	33 043	33 064
33 021	33 044	33 065
33 022		

TOTAL: 64

Class 33/1 Bo-Bo★

Class 33 locomotives fitted for push-pull operation with MU stock
Buckeye couplers
Weight: 77½ tons
Previous no. series: Random from D6511–6580

33 101	33 108	33 114
33 102	33 109	33 115
33 103	33 110	33 116
33 104	33 111	33 117
33 105	33 112	33 118
33 106	33 113	33 119
33 107		

TOTAL: 19

Class 33/2 Bo-Bo★

Class 33 locomotives with narrow (8′ 8″) body for Hastings line
Weight: 76½ tons
Previous no. series: D6586–6597

33 201	33 205	33 209
33 202	33 206	33 210
33 203	33 207	33 211
33 204	33 208	33 212

TOTAL: 12

Class 37 Co-Co★

Built 1960–65
Engine: English Electric 12-cyl. 12CSVT of 1,750 b.h.p. (1,306 kW)
Mechanical parts: English Electric
Weight: 101–6 tons
Brake force: 58 tons. Vacuum brake (¶dual braked)
Maximum tractive effort: 55,500 lb
Power/control equipment: English Electric. Six EE 538 traction motors
Some fitted with steam heating
Previous no. series: D6600–6608, D6700–6999

37 001¶	37 007¶	37 013
37 002¶	37 008¶	37 014¶
37 003	37 009	37 015
37 004¶	37 010¶	37 016¶
37 005	37 011	37 017
37 006¶	37 012¶	37 018¶

Class 33/1 Bo-Bo No. 33 104 [*N. E. Preedy*

37 019¶
37 020¶
37 021¶
37 022¶
37 023
37 024¶
37 025
37 026¶
37 027¶
37 028
37 029
37 030¶
37 031¶
37 032
37 033¶
37 034¶
37 035
37 036
37 037¶
37 038
37 039¶
37 040
37 041¶
37 042¶
37 043¶
37 044¶
37 045¶
37 046
37 047¶
37 048
37 049¶
37 050¶
37 051
37 052¶
37 053
37 054
37 055¶
37 056¶
37 057¶
37 058
37 059¶
37 060¶
37 061
37 062
37 063
37 064¶
37 065
37 066
37 067¶
37 068¶
37 069¶
37 070¶
37 071
37 072¶
37 073¶
37 074¶
37 075
37 076¶
37 077¶
37 078¶
37 079
37 080¶
37 081¶
37 082
37 083
37 084¶
37 085¶
37 086¶
37 087
37 088¶
37 089¶
37 090
37 091¶
37 092
37 093
37 094
37 095¶
37 096
37 097
37 098
37 099
37 100
37 101
37 102
37 103¶
37 104
37 105¶
37 106
37 107
37 108¶
37 109
37 110
37 111¶
37 112¶
37 113
37 114
37 115¶
37 116¶
37 117
37 118¶
37 119¶
37 120¶
37 121¶
37 122¶
37 123¶
37 124¶
37 125¶
37 126¶
37 127¶
37 128¶
37 129¶
37 130¶
37 131¶
37 132¶
37 133¶
37 134¶
37 135¶
37 136¶
37 137¶
37 138¶
37 139¶
37 140¶
37 141¶
37 142¶
37 143¶
37 144¶
37 145¶
37 146¶
37 147¶
37 148¶
37 149¶
37 150¶
37 151¶
37 152¶
37 153¶
37 154¶
37 155¶
37 156¶
37 157¶
37 158¶
37 159¶
37 160¶
37 161¶
37 162
37 163¶
37 164¶
37 165¶
37 166¶
37 167¶
37 168¶
37 169¶
37 170¶
37 171¶
37 172¶
37 173¶
37 174¶
37 175¶
37 176¶
37 177‡¶
37 178¶
37 179¶
37 180¶
37 181¶
37 182¶
37 183¶
37 184¶
37 185‡¶
37 186¶
37 187¶
37 188¶
37 189¶
37 190¶
37 191¶
37 192¶
37 193¶
37 194¶
37 195¶
37 196
37 197¶
37 198¶
37 199¶
37 200¶
37 201¶
37 202¶
37 203¶
37 204
37 205¶
37 206¶
37 207¶
37 208¶
37 209§¶
37 210¶
37 211¶
37 212¶
37 213
37 214
37 215¶
37 216¶
37 217
37 218
37 219¶
37 220
37 221¶
37 222
37 223
37 224¶
37 225
37 226¶
37 227
37 228
37 229
37 230
37 231¶
37 232¶
37 233¶
37 234¶
37 235§
37 236¶
37 237¶
37 238¶
37 239
37 240
37 241¶
37 242¶
37 243¶
37 244¶
37 245¶
37 246¶
37 247¶
37 248
37 249¶
37 250¶
37 251
37 252¶
37 253
37 254¶
37 255¶
37 256¶
37 257¶
37 258¶
37 259¶
37 260¶
37 261¶
37 262¶
37 263¶
37 264¶
37 265¶
37 266¶
37 267¶
37 268¶
37 269¶
37 270¶
37 271¶
37 272¶
37 273¶
37 274¶
37 275¶
37 276¶
37 277¶
37 278¶
37 279¶
37 280¶
37 281¶
37 282¶
37 283¶
37 284¶
37 285¶
37 286¶
37 287¶
37 288¶
37 289¶
37 290¶
37 291¶
37 292¶
37 293¶
37 294¶
37 295¶
37 296¶
37 297¶
37 298¶
37 299¶
37 300¶
37 301¶
37 302¶
37 303¶
37 304¶
37 305¶
37 306¶
37 307¶
37 308¶

TOTAL: 308

Class 40 1Co-Co1★

Built 1958–62
Engine: English Electric 16-cyl. 16SVT Mk. 2 of 2,000 b.h.p. (1,492 kW)
Mechanical parts: English Electric
Weight: 128–34 tons
Brake force: 86 tons. Vacuum brake (¶dual braked)
Maximum tractive effort: 52,000 lb
Power/control equipment: English Electric. Six EE 526/5D traction motors
Route availability: 6
Maximum speed: 90 m.p.h.
Steam heating (some removed)
Previous no. series: D200–399

40 001¶ 40 004¶ 40 008
40 002¶ 40 006¶ 40 009
40 003 40 007¶
40 010 Empress of Britain
40 011 Mauretania
40 012¶ Aureol
40 013¶ Andania
40 014¶ Antonia
40 015¶ Aquitania
40 016¶ Campania
40 017 Carinthia
40 018 Carmania
40 019 Caronia
40 020 Franconia
40 022¶ Laconia
40 023 Lancastria
40 024¶ Lucania
40 025¶ Lusitania

40 026

40 027¶ Parthia
40 028¶ Samaria
40 029¶ Saxonia
40 030¶ Scythia
40 031 Sylvania
40 032 Empress of Canada
40 033¶ Empress of England
40 034¶ Accra
40 035¶ Apapa

40 036 40 038¶ 40 042
40 037 40 040 40 044¶

40 046
40 047¶
40 049
40 050¶
40 051
40 052¶
40 054¶
40 055¶
40 056¶
40 057¶
40 058¶
40 060¶
40 061¶
40 062
40 063¶
40 064¶
40 065
40 066¶
40 067¶
40 068¶
40 069¶
40 070
40 071¶
40 073¶
40 074¶
40 075
40 076¶
40 077¶
40 078¶
40 079¶
40 080¶
40 081¶
40 082¶
40 083¶
40 084¶
40 085¶
40 086¶
40 087
40 088
40 090¶
40 091¶
40 092
40 093¶
40 094¶
40 095¶
40 096¶
40 097¶
40 098¶
40 099¶
40 100
40 101
40 103¶
40 104¶
40 105
40 106
40 107
40 108
40 109
40 110¶
40 111¶
40 112
40 113¶
40 114
40 115
40 116¶
40 117¶
40 118¶
40 119¶
40 120
40 121
40 122¶
40 123
40 124¶
40 125
40 126¶
40 127¶
40 128¶
40 129¶
40 130¶
40 131¶
40 132¶
40 133¶
40 134¶
40 135
40 136¶
40 137¶
40 138
40 139¶
40 140¶
40 141¶
40 142
40 143¶
40 144
40 145¶
40 146¶
40 147¶
40 148
40 149¶
40 150¶
40 151¶
40 152¶
40 153¶
40 154¶
40 155¶
40 156
40 157¶
40 158¶
40 159¶
40 160¶
40 161
40 162¶
40 163¶
40 164¶
40 165¶
40 166¶
40 167¶
40 168¶
40 169¶
40 170¶
40 171¶
40 172¶
40 173
40 174¶
40 175
40 176¶
40 177¶
40 178¶
40 179
40 180¶
40 181¶
40 182¶
40 183
40 184
40 185¶
40 186¶
40 187
40 188¶
40 191¶
40 192¶
40 193¶
40 194¶
40 195¶
40 196¶
40 197¶
40 198
40 199¶

TOTAL: 185

Class 37 Bo-Bo No. 37 043 [*B. J. Nicolle*

Class 37 Bo-Bo No. 37 290 [*N. E. Preedy*

Class 44 1Co-Co1★

"Peak" Class. Introduced 1959
Engine: Sulzer 12-cyl. 12LDA28-A of 2,300 b.h.p. (1,715 kW)
Mechanical parts: BR
Weight: 133 tons
Brake force: 108 tons. Vacuum brake
Maximum tractive effort: 50,000 lb
Power/control equipment: Crompton Parkinson. Six CP171 B1 traction motors
Route availability: 7
Maximum speed: 90 m.p.h.
No train heating
Previous no. series: D1–10

44 002 Helvellyn
44 004 Great Gable
44 005 Cross Fell
44 007 Ingleborough
44 008 Penyghent
44 009 Snowdon
Scheduled for early withdrawal

TOTAL: 6

Class 45 1Co-Co1★

Uprated development of "Peak" Class, built 1960–2
Engine: Sulzer 12-cyl. 12LDA28-B of 2,500 b.h.p. (1,865 kW)
Mechanical parts: BR
Weight: 135 tons
Brake force: 107 tons. Dual braked
Maximum tractive effort: 55,000 lb
Power/control equipment: Crompton Parkinson. Six CP C172 A1 traction motors
Route availability: 7
Maximum speed: 90 m.p.h.
Steam heating
Previous no. series: Random from D11–137

Class 45/0

45 001	45 002	45 003

45 004 Royal Irish Fusilier

45 005

45 006 Honourable Artillery Company

45 007	45 010	45 012
45 008	45 011	45 013
45 009		

45 014 The Cheshire Regiment

45 015	45 018	45 020
45 016	45 019	45 021
45 017		

45 022 Lytham St. Annes
45 023 The Royal Pioneer Corps

45 024	45 029	45 034
45 025	45 030	45 035
45 026	45 031	45 036
45 027	45 032	45 037
45 028	45 033	45 038

45 039 The Manchester Regiment
45 040 King's Shropshire Light Infantry
45 041 Royal Tank Regiment

45 042

45 043 The King's Own Royal Border Regiment
45 044 Royal Inniskilling Fusilier
45 045 Coldstream Guardsman
45 046 Royal Fusilier

45 047

45 048 The Royal Marines
45 049 The Staffordshire Regiment (The Prince of Wales's)

45 050	45 052	45 054
45 051	45 053	

45 055 Royal Corps of Transport

45 056	45 057	45 058

45 059 Royal Engineer
45 060 Sherwood Forester

45 061	45 064	45 068
45 062	45 065	45 069
45 063	45 066	45 070

Class 40 1Co-Co1 No. 40 056 [N. E. Preedy

Class 40 1Co-Co1 No. 40 106 in green livery [B. J. Nicolle

45 071	45 074	45 076
45 072	45 075	45 077
45 073		

TOTAL: 76

Class 45/1 1Co-Co1★

Class 45/0 without steam heating
Weight: 133 tons
Dual braked
Electric train heating equipment
Previous no. series:
Random from D11–137

45 101	45 102	45 103

45 104 The Royal Warwickshire Fusilier

45 105	45 107	45 109
45 106	45 108	45 110

45 111 Grenadier Guardsman
45 112 Royal Army Ordnance Corps

45 113	45 115	45 117
45 114	45 116	

45 118 The Royal Artilleryman

45 119	45 121	45 122
45 120		

45 123 The Lancashire Fusilier

45 124	45 128	45 132
45 125	45 129	45 133
45 126	45 130	45 134
45 127	45 131	

45 135 3rd Carabinier

45 136

45 137 The Bedfordshire and Hertfordshire Regiment (T.A.)

45 138	45 140	45 142
45 139	45 141	

45 143 5th Royal Inniskilling Dragoon Guards
45 144 Royal Signals

45 145	45 148
45 146	45 149
45 147	45 150 (45 054)

TOTAL: 50

Class 46 1Co-Co1★

Introduced 1961. Final development of "Peak" Class
Engine: Sulzer 12-cyl. 12LDA28-B of 2,500 b.h.p. (1,865 kW)
Mechanical parts: BR
Weight: 138 tons
Brake force: 107 tons. Dual braked
Maximum tractive effort: 55,000 lb
Power/control equipment: Brush. Six TM 73–68 Mk. 3 traction motors
Route availability: 7
Maximum speed: 90 m.p.h.
Steam heating
Previous no. series: D138–193

46 001	46 010	46 019
46 002	46 011	46 020
46 003	46 012	46 021
46 004	46 013	46 022
46 005	46 014	46 023
46 006	46 015	46 024
46 007	46 016	46 025
46 008	46 017	
46 009	46 018	

46 026 Leicestershire and Derbyshire Yeomanry

46 027	46 037	46 047
46 028	46 038	46 048
46 029	46 039	46 049
46 030	46 040	46 050
46 031	46 041	46 051
46 032	46 042	46 052
46 033	46 043	46 053
46 034	46 044	46 054
46 035	46 045	46 055
46 036	46 046	46 056

TOTAL: 56

Class 44 1Co-Co1 No. 44 009 Snowdon [*B. Morrison*

Class 45 1Co-Co1 No. 45 041 Royal Tank Regiment [*B. J. Nicolle*

Class 46 1Co-Co1 No. 46 013

[*B. J. Nicolle*

Class 47 Co-Co

Built 1962–7
Engine: Sulzer 12-cyl. 12LDA28-C of 2,580 b.h.p. (1,925 kW) (not 47 601)
Weight: 109–23 tons
Brake force: 101 tons. Dual braked
Maximum tractive effort: 62,000 lb (47 401–20 55,000 lb) (47 601 57,325 lb)
Power/control equipment: Brush. Six TM 64–68 Mk. 1 or Mk. 1A traction motors
Route availability: 6
Maximum speed: 95 m.p.h.
Steam heating. Some isolated
Previous no. series: Random from D1500–1999, D1100–1111

Class 47/0

47 001	47 026	47 048
47 002	47 027	47 049
47 003	47 028	47 050
47 004	47 029	47 051
47 005	47 030	47 052
47 006	47 031	47 053
47 007	47 032	47 054
47 008	47 033	47 055
47 009	47 034	47 056
47 010	47 035	47 059
47 011	47 036	47 060
47 012	47 037	47 061
47 013	47 038	47 063
47 014	47 039	47 064
47 015	47 040	47 066
47 016	47 041	47 068
47 017	47 042	47 069
47 018	47 043	47 070
47 019	47 044	47 072
47 020	47 045	47 074
47 024	47 047	47 075

47 076 City of Truro
47 077 North Star
47 078 Sir Daniel Gooch
47 079 George Jackson Churchward
47 080 Titan
47 081 Odin
47 082 Atlas
47 083 Orion
47 085 Mammoth
47 086 Colossus
47 087 Cyclops
47 088 Samson
47 089 Amazon
47 090 Vulcan
47 091 Thor

47 093	47 138	47 183
47 094	47 140	47 184
47 095	47 141	47 185
47 096	47 142	47 186
47 097	47 143	47 187
47 098	47 144	47 188
47 099	47 145	47 189
47 100	47 146	47 190
47 101	47 147	47 191
47 102	47 148	47 192
47 103	47 149	47 193
47 104	47 150	47 194
47 105	47 151	47 195
47 106	47 152	47 196
47 107	47 155	47 197
47 108	47 156	47 198
47 109	47 157	47 199
47 110	47 158	47 200
47 111	47 159	47 201
47 112	47 160	47 202
47 113	47 162	47 203
47 114	47 163	47 204
47 115	47 164	47 205
47 116	47 165	47 206
47 117	47 166	47 207
47 118	47 167	47 208
47 119	47 168	47 209
47 120	47 169	47 210
47 121	47 170	47 211
47 122	47 171	47 212
47 123	47 172	47 213
47 124	47 173	47 214
47 125	47 174	47 215
47 128	47 175	47 216
47 129	47 176	47 217
47 130	47 177	47 218
47 131	47 178	47 219
47 134	47 179	47 220
47 135	47 180	47 221
47 136	47 181	47 222
47 137	47 182	47 223

Class 47 Co-Co No. 47 183 [*C. J. Leigh*

47 224	47 248	47 276
47 225	47 249	47 277
47 226	47 250	47 278
47 227	47 251	47 279
47 228	47 252	47 280
47 229	47 254	47 281
47 230	47 255	47 282
47 231	47 256	47 283
47 232	47 257	47 284
47 233	47 258	47 285
47 234	47 262	47 286
47 235	47 263	47 287
47 236	47 264	47 288
47 237	47 265	47 289
47 238	47 266	47 290
47 239	47 267	47 291
47 240	47 268	47 292
47 241	47 269	47 293
47 242	47 270	47 294
47 243	47 271	47 295
47 244	47 272	47 296
47 245	47 273	47 297
47 246	47 274	47 298
47 247	47 275	

TOTAL: 272

Class 47/3 **Co-Co**

Class 47 locomotives without train heating

Weight: 112 tons

Previous no. series: D1782–1900

47 301	47 319	47 337
47 302	47 320	47 338
47 303	47 321	47 339
47 304	47 322	47 340
47 305	47 323	47 341
47 306	47 324	47 342
47 307	47 325	47 343
47 308	47 326	47 344
47 309	47 327	47 345
47 310	47 328	47 346
47 311	47 329	47 347
47 312	47 330	47 348
47 313	47 331	47 349
47 314	47 332	47 350
47 315	47 333	47 351
47 316	47 334	47 352
47 317	47 335	47 353
47 318	47 336	47 354

47 355	47 364	47 373
47 356	47 365	47 374
47 357	47 366	47 375
47 358	47 367	47 376
47 359	47 368	47 377
47 360	47 369	47 378
47 361	47 370	47 379
47 362	47 371	47 380
47 363	47 372	47 381

TOTAL: 81

Class 47/4 **Co-Co**

Class 47 locomotives with electric or dual train heating

Weight: 120–5 tons

Previous no. series: Random from D1500–1999

47 401	47 429	47 457
47 402	47 430	47 458
47 403	47 431	47 459
47 404	47 432	47 460
47 405	47 433	47 461
47 406	47 434	47 462
47 407	47 435	47 463
47 408	47 436	47 464
47 409	47 437	47 465
47 410	47 438	47 466
47 411	47 439	47 467
47 412	47 440	47 468
47 413	47 441	47 469
47 414	47 442	47 470
47 415	47 443	47 471
47 416	47 444	47 472
47 417	47 445	47 473
47 418	47 446	47 474
47 419	47 447	47 475
47 420	47 448	47 476
47 421	47 449	47 477
47 422	47 450	47 478
47 423	47 451	47 479
47 424	47 452	47 480
47 425	47 453	47 481
47 426	47 454	47 482
47 427	47 455	47 483
47 428	47 456	

47 484 Isambard Kingdom Brunel

47 485	47 487	47 489
47 486	47 488	47 490

Class 50 Co-Co No. 50 016 [B. J. Nicolle

47 491	47 507	47 523
47 492	47 508	47 524
47 493	47 509	47 525
47 494	47 510	47 526
47 495	47 511	47 527
47 496	47 512	47 528
47 497	47 513	47 529
47 498	47 514	47 530
47 499	47 515	47 531
47 500	47 516	47 532
47 501	47 517	47 533
47 502	47 518	47 534
47 503	47 519	47 535
47 504	47 520	47 536
47 505	47 521	47 537
47 506	47 522	

47 538 Python

47 539	47 547
47 540	47 549
47 541	47 550
47 542	47 551 (47 153)
47 543	47 552
47 544	47 553 (47 260)
47 545	47 554
47 546	47 555 (47 126)

TOTAL: 154

Class 47/6 Co-Co

Class 47 locomotive re-engined
Engine: Ruston Paxman 16 RK 3CT 3,250 h.p. (2,460 kW)
Weight: 116 tons
Previous no. series: D1628

47 601 (47 046)

TOTAL: 1

Class 50 Co-Co■

Built 1967–8. Originally leased to BR.
Engine: English Electric 16-cyl. 16CSVT of 2,700 b.h.p. (2,014 kW)
Mechanical parts: English Electric
Weight: 115 tons
Brake force: 99 tons. Dual braked
Maximum tractive effort: 48,500 lb
Power/control equipment: English Electric. Six 538/5A traction motors
Route availability: 6
Maximum speed: 100 m.p.h.
Electric train heating only
Previous no. series: D400–49

50 001 Dreadnought
50 002 Superb
50 003 Temeraire
50 004 St. Vincent
50 005 Collingwood
50 006 Neptune
50 007 Hercules
50 008 Thunderer
50 009 Conqueror
50 010 Monarch
50 011 Centurion
50 012 Benbow
50 013 Agincourt
50 014 Warspite
50 015 Valiant
50 016 Barham
50 017 Royal Oak
50 018 Resolution
50 019 Ramillies
50 020 Revenge
50 021 Rodney
50 022 Anson
50 023 Howe
50 024 Vanguard
50 025 Invincible
50 026 Indomitable
50 027 Lion
50 028 Tiger
50 029 Renown
50 030 Repulse
50 031 Hood
50 032 Courageous
50 033 Glorious
50 034 Furious
50 035 Ark Royal
50 036 Victorious
50 037 Illustrious
50 038 Formidable
50 039 Implacable
50 040 Leviathan
50 041 Bulwark
50 042 Triumph

50 043	Eagle
50 044	Exeter
50 045	Achilles
50 046	Ajax
50 047	Swiftsure
50 048	Dauntless
50 049	Defiance
50 050	Fearless

Nameplates may not yet be fitted to some

TOTAL: 50

Class 55 Co-Co

Introduced 1961. Production version of "Deltic" prototype locomotive
Engines: Two 18-cyl. Napier "Deltic" 18–25 of 1,650 b.h.p. Total 3,300 b.h.p. (2,462 kW)
Mechanical parts: English Electric
Weight: 103 tons
Brake force: 87 tons. Dual braked
Maximum tractive effort: 50.000 lb
Power/control equipment: English Electric. Six EE 538 traction motors
Route availability: 5
Maximum speed: 100 m.p.h.
Fitted with dual train-heating equipment
Previous no. series: D9000–9021

55 001	St. Paddy
55 002	The King's Own Yorkshire Light Infantry
55 003	Meld
55 004	Queen's Own Highlander
55 005	The Prince of Wales's Own Regiment of Yorkshire
55 006	The Fife & Forfar Yeomanry
55 007	Pinza
55 008	The Green Howards
55 009	Alycidon
55 010	The King's Own Scottish Borderer
55 011	The Royal Northumberland Fusiliers
55 012	Crepello
55 013	The Black Watch
55 014	The Duke of Wellington's Regiment
55 015	Tulyar
55 016	Gordon Highlander
55 017	The Durham Light Infantry
55 018	Ballymoss
55 019	Royal Highland Fusilier
55 020	Nimbus
55 021	Argyll & Sutherland Highlander
55 022	Royal Scots Grey

TOTAL: 22

Class 56 Co-Co

Introduced 1976. Still in production. Nos. 56 001–30 built in Romania; 56 031–90 built BREL
Engine: GEC Diesels 16-cyl. 16RK3CT of 3,250 b.h.p. (2,460 kW)
Mechanical parts: BR/Brush/Electroputere
Weight: 126 tons
Brake force: 84 tons. Air braked
Maximum tractive effort: 49,456 lb
Power/control equipment: Brush. Six TM 76–32 traction motors
Route availability: 7
Maximum speed: 80 m.p.h.
No train heating

56 001	56 016	56 031
56 002	56 017	56 032
56 003	56 018	56 033
56 004	56 019	56 034
56 005	56 020	56 035
56 006	56 021	56 036
56 007	56 022	56 037
56 008	56 023	56 038
56 009	56 024	56 039
56 010	56 025	56 040
56 011	56 026	56 041
56 012	56 027	56 042
56 013	56 028	56 043
56 014	56 029	56 044
56 015	56 030	56 045

Class 55 Co-Co No. 55 010 The King's Own Scottish Borderer [*B. J. Nicolle*

Class 56 Co-Co No. 56 016 [*N. E. Preedy*

Class 253 power car No. W43033 [*R. E. Ruffell*

56 046	56 061	56 076
56 047	56 062	56 077
56 048	56 063	56 078
56 049	56 064	56 079
56 050	56 065	56 080
56 051	56 066	56 081
56 052	56 067	56 082
56 053	56 068	56 083
56 054	56 069	56 084
56 055	56 070	56 085
56 056	56 071	56 086
56 057	56 072	56 087
56 058	56 073	56 088
56 059	56 074	56 089
56 060	56 075	56 090

Class 253

Power cars for High Speed Train. Built 1976–7 for Western Region London–Bristol/South Wales services. Fourteen further units on order for WR. Used as pairs with Mk. III coaches coupled between them in units 253 001–27. Complete units listed in DMU section

Engine: Paxman Valenta 12-cyl. 12RP200L V-type of 2,250 b.h.p. (1,680 kW)

Mechanical parts: BREL

Weight: 66 tons

Power/control equipment: Brush. Four traction motors driving through a cardan shaft with flexible couplings and single reduction gearing

Maximum speed: 125 m.p.h.

W43002	W43013	W43024
W43003	W43014	W43025
W43004	W43015	W43026
W43005	W43016	W43027
W43006	W43017	W43028
W43007	W43018	W43029
W43008	W43019	W43030
W43009	W43020	W43031
W43010	W43021	W43032
W43011	W43022	W43033
W43012	W43023	W43034
W43035	W43042	W43049
W43036	W43043	W43050
W43037	W43044	W43051
W43038	W43045	W43052
W43039	W43046	W43053
W43040	W43047	W43054
W43041	W43048	W43055

TOTAL: 54

Class 254

Power cars for High Speed Train. Introduced 1977 for Eastern Region East Coast main line services. Used in pairs with Mk. III coaches coupled between them in units 254 001–32* Complete units listed in DMU section

Engine: Paxman Valenta 12-cyl. 12RP200L V-type of 2,250 b.h.p. (1680 kW)

Mechanical parts: BREL

Weight: 66 tons

Power/control equipment: Brush. Four traction motors driving through a cardan shaft with flexible couplings and single reduction gearing

Maximum speed: 125 m.p.h.

E43056	E43075	E43094
E43057	E43076	E43095
E43058	E43077	E43096
E43059	E43078	E43097
E43060	E43079	E43098
E43061	E43080	E43099
E43062	E43081	E43100
E43063	E43082	E43101
E43064	E43083	E43102
E43065	E43084	E43103
E43066	E43085	E43104
E43067	E43086	E43105
E43068	E43087	E43106
E43069	E43088	E43107
E43070	E43089	E43108
E43071	E43090	E43109
E43072	E43091	E43110
E43073	E43092	E43111
E43074	E43093	E43112

E43113	E43117	W43121*	*Spare power cars for WR Class 253 sets delivered 1977
E43114	E43118	E43122	
E43115	E43119	E43123	
E43116	W43120*		

TOTAL: 68

DEPARTMENTAL LOCOMOTIVES

Departmental locomotives are not shown in official stock change lists. These notes represent the latest known position.

Former numbers in brackets

Class 42 B-B

Former "Warship" Class diesel hydraulic locomotives built at Swindon in 1958. Not self-propelled; 832 now used as dead-load vehicle at Derby Research Department. 818 retained for spares at Swindon
Weight: 80 tons
Vacuum braked
818 Glory 832 Onslaught

Class 08 0-6-0

Snow ploughs, converted from Class 08 locomotives
Not self-propelled. Further units being converted

ADB966506 (3078)
ADB966507 (3006)
ADB966508 (3035)
ADB966509 (3069)
ADB966510 (3037)

Class 24/1 Bo-Bo★

For details see Class 24

Test-train locomotive
RDB968007 (24 061)

Train pre-heating units
TDB 968008 (24 054)
TDB 968009 (24 142)

Class 28 Co-Bo ●

Introduced 1958
Train pre-heating unit converted from former Metro-Vick 1,200 b.h.p. locomotive

TDB968006 (S15705, D5705)

Class 35 B-B △

Former "Hymek" Class diesel hydraulic locomotives built by Beyer-Peacock in 1961. Not self-propelled. Retained as dead-load vehicles at Derby

7076 7096

Classes 17/1 and *17/3 ♦ Clayton & *Beyer-Peacock Bo-Bo

Introduced 1962. Retained at Derby Research Department. S18521 for spares only
Engines Two Paxman 6-cyl. 6ZHXL of 450 b.h.p. at 1,500 r.p.m. Total (671 kW)
Weight: 68 tons
Maximum tractive effort: 40,000 lb

Departmental Class 42 B-B No. 818 Glory (non-operable) [*B. J. Nicolle*

Ruston & Hornsby 0-6-0 departmental shunter No. PWM 650 [*B. J. Nicolle*

Transmission: Electric. Four GEC (*Crompton Parkinson) axle-hung nose-suspended traction motors

S18521 (8521) 8598*

Class 15 Bo-Bo

Non-powered carriage-heating units, converted from Class 15 locomotives

DB968000 (8243)
DB968001 (8233)
DB968002 (8237)
DB968003 (8203)

Ruston & Hornsby 0-4-0 Shunter

Introduced: 1957
Engine: Ruston & Hornsby 4-cyl. of 88 b.h.p. (68 kW)
Weight: 17 tons.
Maximum tractive effort: 9,500 lb
Transmission: Mechanical. Chain driven from gear-box
Route availability: 1

20

Ruston & Hornsby 0-6-0 Shunter

Introduced: 1953
Engine: Ruston & Hornsby 6-cyl. of 165 b.h.p. (124 kW)
Weight: 30 tons
Maximum tractive effort: 17,000 lb
Transmission: Electric: One BTH nose-suspended traction motor
Route availability: 1

PWM650 PWM653
PWM651 PWM654
PWM652

LATE INFORMATION

This list is correct to 31 December.

Locomotives withdrawn: 08 003/10/25/43/8/70, 08 144/5, 08 229/67, 08 306/7, 46 005.

Air brakes: 08 388.

Dual brakes: 25 323/5, 37 015, 37 094.

STEAMTOWN RAILWAY MUSEUM
Warton Road, Carnforth, Lancs

STEAMTOWN
RAILWAY MUSEUM LTD.

Associated with FLYING SCOTSMAN ENTERPRISES

The Steam Railway Museum and Leisure Centre of the North West

HOW TO GET THERE By rail, or by road via M6 and A6

LOCOMOTIVES

British Main Line

44871	LMS Class 5 (built Crewe)
44932	LMS Class 5 (built Horwich 1945)
45407	LMS Class 5 (built Armstrong Whitworth 1938)
6441	LMS Class 2MT (built Crewe 1950)
1306	LNER Class B1 *Mayflower* (built NB Loco Co, Glasgow 1947)
4472	LNER Class A3 *Flying Scotsman* (built Doncaster 1923)
4498	LNER Class A4 *Sir Nigel Gresley* (built Doncaster 1935)
5643	0–6–2 Tank Locomotive 56XX Class (built Swindon 1925)
35005	SR Merchant Navy Class *Canadian Pacific* (built Eastleigh 1941)
1122	Lancashire & Yorkshire 0–6–0 Tender Loco (built Horwich 1891)
850	Southern Railway *Lord Nelson* (built Eastleigh 1927)

Continental Main Line

231K22	French National Railways (SNCF) Compound 4–6–2 (built 1914)
01 1104	German Federal Railways (DB) Oil fired 4–6–2 (built 1940)
80 014	German Federal Railways (DB) 0–6–0 Tank (built 1928)

British Industrial

Cranford No 2 Bagnall 0–6–0 ST (built 1942, Works No 2668)

COACHES

CR41	Caledonian Railway Observation (built 1897)
NE305	NER Directors' Saloon (built 1902)
GN397	GNR Officers' Saloon (built 1912)
GE1	GER Chairman's Saloon (built 1920)
24287	LNER Gresley Buffet (built 1930)
9004	GWR Officers' Saloon (built 1930)
M395	LMS Sleeping Car
Pullman's	*Rosalind* and *Zena*

FURTHER ATTRACTIONS

A Midland Railway signal box, model railway, coaling plant, 15 in. gauge railway, other industrial locos and cranes, Café, gift shop and Collectors' Corner.

Admission to Steamtown covers all listed attractions including unlimited rides when locos are in steam.

OPEN DAILY Summer 0900–1800 Winter 0900–1630
Facilities subject to change without notice.

DIESEL MULTIPLE-UNITS

BR diesel multiple units currently in service were mostly built between 1955 and 1963, and although body styles differ there is considerable mechanical standardisation. Some non-standard classes have been withdrawn in recent years, although a few odd examples survive in departmental use. The most recent withdrawals are of Class 125/1, 125/2, and 185 vehicles with hydraulic transmission (incompatible with other classes) which were displaced by 25kV electrification of the ER GN Suburban lines. Most dmu vehicles are likely to be retained until about 1990, and with this in mind, cars of several classes are being refurbished. Many of these are appearing in the revised livery of white with a blue stripe and some bear the insignia of the relevant Passenger Transport Executive. Gloucester and Swindon-built cross-country units are having their BUT/AEC engines replaced with the more powerful Leyland 0680. Refurbished vehicles are denoted by a letter "R" adjacent to the number in this publication.

Withdrawals are confined in the main to accident-damaged vehicles or the removal of certain surplus types. In this latter category, Gloucester Class 100, and Park Royal Class 103 vehicles are likely to be withdrawn as soon as they become surplus. BRCW and Cravens Classes 105/1, 105/2, 140, 141 and 160 are all scheduled for possible withdrawal before 1985. The Swindon-built Trans-Pennine units, some BRCW, Derby, Gloucester and Metro-Cammell units and all the SR diesel-electric units are likely to be replaced from 1985 to 1990.

New additions have been confined to power cars and Mk.3 coaches for High Speed Trains. These have comprised the last Class 253 units of the 27 on order for the WR, and the first of the ER allocation of Class 254 units. These latest power cars have engines rated at 2.250 h.p. as on the earlier units and have not been uprated as originally planned. The Class 254 units have detailed equipment differences and each set has an extra second class trailer. Fourteen further Class 253 units have been ordered for WR West of England services. HST units are listed by unit numbers in this publication, and the power cars are also shown separately under their individual numbers in the diesel locomotives section.

Unless otherwise stated, all multiple-unit trains are gangwayed within each set, with guard's and luggage compartment at the inner end of motor brake coaches, and seating is in open saloons with centre and/or end doors. The letter (L) in the headings indicates an open vehicle fitted with toilet facilities; (K) indicates a side corridor vehicle with toilet. Two standard lengths of underframe are in use, namely 56 ft. 11 in. and 63 ft. 5 in., but the actual body lengths vary by a few inches for the same type of underframe. The dimensions shown are the length over body and the overall width.

Cars are listed in numerical order by type and not by set formation. Several of the types listed are sub-divided by reason of detail or mechanical differences. For example, a certain number of cars in a class may have different seating arrangement or a different make of engine but are otherwise similar to the main batch. Such differences are noted in the heading to the class and given a reference mark by which the relevant dimensions or details and the cars concerned can be identified.

The type of set in which each class is usually formed, together with the principal manufacturer, is shown at the head of the details for that class, although it should be noted that changes may occur owing to varying operating conditions, even to the extent of coupling different makes of car in the same set or running power cars without intermediate trailers.

Most railcars are fitted with a standard mechanical transmission of a cardan shaft and freewheel to a four-speed epicyclic gearbox, and a further cardan shaft to the final drive. Where a non-standard transmission is employed, details are shown under the relevant heading.

The numbers of diesel multiple-units in service have been checked to the following dates: ER 2 October, ScR 29 October, LMR 1 October, SR 3 October, WR 8 October. See also "Late Information" section.

Alterations to multiple-unit stock, together with information for updating this book, is shown in the Locomotive Stock Changes section of the Ian Allan monthly magazines *Modern Railways* and *Railway World*.

COUPLING CODES

Although several multiple-unit diesel sets can be coupled together and driven by one man in the leading cab, for various reasons it is not possible for all types of diesel unit to work together. In order to distinguish cars that can run together, all have painted at each end above the buffers a colour code symbol. A miniature symbol also appears on the plug socket covers. Only units bearing the same symbol may be coupled together.

★ ORANGE STAR
♦ YELLOW DIAMOND
▲ RED TRIANGLE
● WHITE CIRCLE
■ BLUE SQUARE

Class 114 (2)■

Derby Works, B.R.

Motor Brake Second

Introduced: 1956

Engines:

Two B.U.T. (Leyland Albion) 6-cyl. horizontal type of 230 b.h.p.

Body: 64′ 6″ × 9′ 3″

Weight: 37 tons 10 cwt

Seats: 2nd, 62

Works with Class 148

E50001	E50016	E50033
E50002	E50017	E50035
E50003	E50018R	E50036
E50004	E50019	E50037
E50005	E50020	E50038R
E50006	E50021	E50039
E50007	E50022	E50040
E50008	E50023	E50041
E50009	E50024	E50042
E50010	E50025	E50043
E50011	E50026	E50044
E50012	E50027	E50045
E50013	E50030	E50046
E50014	E50031	E50047
E50015	E50032	E50049

Class 116/2 (†130) (3 Suburban)■

Derby Works B.R.

Motor Brake Second

Introduced: 1957

Engines:

Two B.U.T. (Leyland) 6-cyl. horizontal types of 150 b.h.p.

Body: 64′ 0″ × 9′ 3″. Non-gangwayed (*gangwayed), with side doors to each seating bay (†converted for parcels traffic)

Weight: 36 tons

Seats: 2nd, 65

Works with Classes 116/1 and 175

M50050	M50051R	M50052R
M50053	M50066	M50079
M50054	M50067	W50080*R
M50055	M50068	M50081*
M50056	M50069	M50082*
M50057	M50070R	W50083*
M50058R	M50071	W50084*
M50059	M50072R	W50086*R
M50060	M50073	W50087*R
M50061R	M50074	W50088*
M50062	M50075	W50089*R
M50063	M50076R	M50090*
M50064R	M50077R	W50091*
M50065R	M50078	

Class 116/1 (†130) (3 Suburban)■

Derby Works, B.R.

Motor Second

Introduced: 1957

Engines:

Two B.U.T. (Leyland) 6-cyl. horizontal type of 150 b.h.p.

Body: 64′ 0″ × 9′ 3″. Non-gangwayed (*gangwayed), with side doors to each seating bay (†converted for parcels traffic)

Weight: 36 tons

Seats: 2nd, 95 (*89)

Works with Classes 116/2 and 175

M50092R	M50107R	M50120R
M50093	M50108	M50121
M50094R	M50109	W50122*R
M50095R	M50110	M50123*
M50097R	M50111	M50124*
M50098	M50112	W50126*
M50099	M50113R	M50127
M50100	M50114	W50128*R
M50101	M50115R	W50129*R
M50102	M50116	W50130*
M50103	M50117	W50131*R
M50104	M50118R	M50132*
M50105R	M50119	W50133*
M50106		

Class 111/2 **(2)■**
Metropolitan-Cammell
Motor Brake Second
Introduced: 1957
Engines:
Two Rolls-Royce 6-cyl. horizontal type of 180 b.h.p.
Body: 57′ 0″×9′ 3″
Weight: 33 tons
Seats: 2nd, 52
Works with Class 144

E50134R	E50136	E50137R
E50135		

Class 101/1 **(4)■**
Metropolitan-Cammell
Motor Composite (L)
Introduced: 1956
Engines:
Two B.U.T. (A.E.C.) 6-cyl. horizontal type of 150 b.h.p.
Body: 57′ 0″×9′ 3″
Weight: 32 tons
Seats: 1st, 12; **2nd**, 53(45*) †**2nd**, 65
Works with Classes 101/2, 162/4/5/71

E50138*	SC50143*	SC50148*
E50139*	E50144*	E50149*
E50140*R	SC50145*	E50150*
SC50141*	E50146*	E50151*
E50142*	E50147*	

Class 101/2 **(2)■**
Metropolitan-Cammell
Motor Brake Second
Introduced: 1956
Engines:
Two B.U.T. (A.E.C.) 6-cyl. horizontal type of 150 b.h.p.
Body: 57′ 0″×9′ 3″
Weight: 32 tons
Seats: 2nd, 52
Works with Class 144

E50152	E50154	E50156
E50153	E50155R	E50157

Class 101/1 **(2)■**
Metropolitan-Cammell
Motor Composite (†Second) (L)
Introduced: 1956
For details see E50138

SC50158	E50160	E50162
SC50159	E50161R	E50163

Class 101/2 **(2)■**
Metropolitan-Cammell
Motor Brake Second
Introduced: 1957
For details see E50152

E50164	E50166	E50167
E50165		

Class 101/1 **(2‡ or 4)**
Metropolitan-Cammell
Motor Composite (L)
Introduced: 1957
For details see E50138

E50168‡	E50179	E50188
E50169‡R	E50180	M50189
E50170‡	E50181	E50191
E50171‡	E50182	E50192
E50172	E50183	E50193R
SC50174	E50184	SC50194
SC50175	E50185	E50195
SC50176	SC50186R	E50196
E50177	SC50187R	M50197
E50178		

Class 101/2 **(2)■**
Metropolitan-Cammell
Motor Brake Second
Introduced: 1957
For details see E50152

E50198R	M50203	M50208R
E50199	E50204	E50209
E50200	E50205	E50210
E50201	M50206	E50211
E50202R	E50207R	E50212

E50214	E50221	M50228
E50215	E50222	E50229
E50216R	E50223	E50230
E50217R	E50224R	E50231
E50218	E50225	E50232
E50219	E50226R	E50233
E50220	E50227R	

Class 101/1 (4)■
Metropolitan-Cammell
Motor Composite (L)
Introduced: 1957
For details see E50138

SC50234*	E50239*	SC50243*
E50235*	E50240*	E50244*
E50237*	E50241*	SC50245*
E50238*	SC50242*	

Class 101/2 (2)■
Metropolitan-Cammell
Motor Brake Second
Introduced: 1957
For details see E50152

E50246	E50247	E50248

Class 105/2 (4)■
Cravens
Motor Brake Second
Introduced: 1959
Engines:
Two B.U.T. (A.E.C.) 6-cyl. horizontal type of 150 b.h.p.
Body: 57′ 6″ × 9′ 2″
Weight: 30 tons (29 tons*)
Seats: 2nd, 52
Transmission:
Mechanical. Standard

E50249

Class 101/2 (2)■
Metropolitan-Cammell
Motor Brake Second
Introduced: 1957
For details see E50152

E50250	SC50254	E50257R
E50251	E50255	E50258
E50252	E50256	E50259
E50253		

Class 101/1 (2)■
Metropolitan-Cammell
Motor Composite (L)
Introduced: 1957
For details see E50138

E50260	SC50264	E50267R
E50261	E50265	E50268
E50262	E50266	SC50269
E50263		

Class 111/1 (3)■
Metropolitan-Cammell
Motor Composite (L)
Introduced: 1957
Engines:
Two Rolls-Royce 6-cyl. horizontal type of 180 b.h.p.
Body: 57′ 0″ × 9′ 3″
Weight: 33 tons
Seats: 1st, 12; **2nd,** 53
Transmission:
Mechanical. Standard

E50270R	E50274	E50277
E50271	E50275	E50278
E50272	E50276R	E50279
E50273R		

Class 111/2 (3)■
Metropolitan-Cammell
Motor Brake Second
Introduced: 1957
For details see E50134

Gloucester RCW Class 100 motor brake second leading a mixed rake [*J. M. Rickard*

Derby 2-car unit with Class 114 motor brake second leading [*P. H. Hanson*

E50280	E50283	E50287
E50281	E50284	E50288R
E50282	E50286	E50289

Class 101/2 (3 or 2*) ■
Metropolitan-Cammell
Motor Brake Second
Introduced: 1957 (1958†)
For details see E50152

SC50290	M50305†R	M50313†
E50291	M50306†	M50314†
SC50292	M50307†	M50315†
E50293*	M50308†	M50316†
E50294*	M50309†	M50317†R
E50295*	M50310†	M50318†
E50296*R	M50311†	M50319†R
M50303†	M50312†	M50320†
M50304†R		

Class 101/1 († 101/3) (3) ■
Metropolitan-Cammell
Motor Composite († Second) (L)
Introduced: 1958
For details see E50138

M50321†	M50327†R	M50333†
M50322	M50328†	M50334
M50323†	M50329†R	M50335†R
M50324†	M50330	M50336†
M50325†	M50331†	M50337
M50326†	M50332†	M50338†R

Class 100 (2) ■
Gloucester R.C. & W. Co.
Motor Brake Second
Introduced: 1957
Engines:
Two B.U.T. (A.E.C.) 6-cyl. horizontal type of 150 b.h.p.
Body: 57′ 6″ × 9′ 3″
Weight: 30 tons
Seats: 2nd, 52
Work with Class 143
*Fitted with C.A.V. Ltd. automatic gear change equipment

M50340	M50349	M50354
M50342	M50350	M50355
M50343	M50351	M50356
E50346	M50352	M50357
M50348	M50353	M50358*

Class 105/2 (2) ■
Cravens
Motor Brake Second
Introduced: 1956
Engines:
Two B.U.T. (Leyland) 6-cyl. horizontal type of 150 b.h.p.
Body: 57′ 6″ × 9′ 2″
Weight: 29 tons
Seats: 2nd, 52
Work with Class 141

E50359	E50363	E50367
E50360	E50364	E50368
E50361	E50365	E50369
E50362	E50366	E50370

Class 105/2 (2) ■
Cravens
Motor Brake Second
Introduced: 1956
For details see E50249

E50371*	E50379*	M50387*
M50372*	E50380*	M50388*
E50373*	E50381*	M50389*
M50374*	E50382*	M50390*
E50375*	E50383*	M50391*
E50376*	E50384*	M50392*
E50377*	M50385*	M50393*
E50378*	E50386*	

Class 103 (2)■

Park Royal Vehicles

Motor Brake Second

Introduced: 1957
Engines:
Two B.U.T. (A.E.C.) 6-cyl. horizontal type of 150 b.h.p.
Body: 57′ 6″ × 9′ 3″
Weight: 33 tons 10 cwt
Seats: **2nd**, 52
Works with Class 145

M50395	M50401	M50405
M50398	M50402	M50408
M50399	M50403	M50409
M50400	M50404	

Class 104/2 (3)■

Birmingham R. C. & W. Co.

Motor Brake Second

Introduced: 1957
Engines:
Two B.U.T. (Leyland) 6-cyl. horizontal type of 150 b.h.p.
Body: 57′ 6″ × 9′ 3″
Weight: 31 tons
Seats: **2nd**, 52
Works with Classes 104/1 and 169

M50420	M50422	M50423
M50421		

Class 104/1 (* 104/3) (3)■

Birmingham R. C. & W. Co.

Motor Composite (*Second) (L)

Introduced: 1957
Engines:
Two B.U.T. (Leyland) 6-cyl. horizontal type of 150 b.h.p.
Body: 57′ 6″ × 9′ 3″
Weight: 31 tons
Seats: **1st**, 12; **2nd**, 54 (†51), ***2nd**, 66
Works with Classes 104/2 and 169

M50424*	M50426*	M50427*
M50425*		

Class 104/2 (3)■

Birmingham R. C. & W. Co.

Motor Brake Second

Introduced: 1957
For details see M50420

M50428	M50447	M50464
M50429	M50448	M50465
M50430	M50449	M50466
M50431	M50450	M50467
M50432	M50451	M50468
M50433	M50452	M50469
M50434	M50453	M50470
M50435	M50454	M50471
M50436	M50455	M50472
M50437	M50456	M50473
M50439	M50457	M50474
M50440	M50458	M50475
M50442	M50459	M50476
M50443	M50460	M50477
M50444	M50461	M50478
M50445	E50462	M50479
M50446	M50463	

Class 104/1 (104/3*) (3)■

Birmingham R. C. & W. Co.

Motor Composite (*Second) (L)

Introduced: 1957
For details see M50424

M50480*	M50491*	M50502
M50481*	M50492*	M50503
M50482*	M50493	M50504
M50483*	M50494	M50505
M50484*	M50496	M50506
M50485*	M50497*	M50507
M50486*	M50498	M50508
M50487*	M50499	M50509
M50488*	M50500	M50510
M50490	M50501	M50511

Two Birmingham RCW 3-car units on a Blackpool–Manchester working [*D. A. Flitcroft*

M50512	M50520	M50526
M50514	M50521	M50527
M50515	M50522	M50528
M50516	M50523	M50529
M50517	M50524	M50530
M50518	M50525	M50531
M50519		

Class 104/2 (2) ■

Birmingham R. C. & W. Co.

Motor Brake Second

Introduced: 1958
For details see M50420

M50532	M50536	M50539
M50533	M50537	M50540
M50534	M50538	M50541
M50535		

Class 104/1 (4) ■

Birmingham R. C. & W. Co.

Motor Composite (L)

Introduced: 1958
For details see M50424

E50542†	E50560†	E50577†
E50543†	E50561†	E50578†
E50544†	E50562†	E50579†
E50545†	E50563†	E50580†
E50546†	E50564†	E50581†
E50547†	E50565†	E50582†
E50548†	E50566†	E50583†
E50549†	E50567†	E50584†
E50550†	E50568†	E50585†
E50551†	E50570†	E50586†
E50552†	E50571†	E50587†
E50553†	E50572†	E50588†
E50554†	E50573†	E50589†
E50555†	E50574†	E50590†
E50556†	E50575†	E50591†
E50557†	E50576†	E50593†

Class 104/2 (2) ■

Birmingham R. C. & W. Co.

Motor Brake Second

Introduced: 1958
For details see M50420

E50594	E50596	E50598
E50595	E50597	

Class 108/2 (2 or 3*) ■

Derby Works, B.R.

Motor Brake Second

Introduced: 1958
Engines:
Two B.U.T. (Leyland) 6-cyl. horizontal type of 150 b.h.p.
Body: 57′ 6″ × 9′ 2″
Weight: 29 tons
Seats: 2nd, 52
Works with Classes (108/1 and 161*) 142

E50599	E50610	E50621*
E50601	E50612	E50622*
E50602	E50613	E50623*
E50603	E50614	E50624*
E50604	E50616	M50625
E50605	E50617	M50626
E50606	E50618	M50627
E50607	E50619	M50628
E50608	E50620*	M50629
E50609		

Class 108/1 (3* or 4) ■

Derby Works, B.R.

Motor Composite (L)

Introduced: 1958
Engines:
Two B.U.T. (Leyland) 6-cyl. horizontal type of 150 b.h.p.
Body: 57′ 6″ × 9′ 2″
Weight: 28 tons
Seats: 1st, 12; **2nd,** 50 (52†, 53‡)
Works with Classes 108/2 and 142

Derby 2-car unit refurbished in West Yorkshire PTE livery [*B. Morrison*

E50630	E50636	E50642*R
E50631	E50637	E50643*R
E50632	E50638	E50644*R
E50633	E50639	E50645*R
E50634	E50641R	E50646*R
E50635		

Class 120/2 (3 Cross Country) ■
Swindon Works, B.R.
Motor Second (L)
Introduced: 1957
Engines:
Two B.U.T. (A.E.C.) (Leyland*) 6-cyl. horizontal type of 150 b.h.p.
Body: 64′ 6″×9′ 3″
Weight: 36 tons 10 cwt
Seats: **2nd**, 68
Works with Classes 120/1 and 179

W50647	M50663	W50679
W50648	W50664	M50680
W50649	W50665	W50681
M50650	W50666	W50682
M50651	M50667	W50683
M50652	W50668	M50684
W50653	M50669	M50685
M50654	M50670	W50686
M50655	M50671	M50687
M50656	W50672	M50688
M50657	W50673	M50689
W50658	W50674*	W50691
W50659	W50675	M50692
W50660	M50676	W50693
W50661	M50677	W50694
W50662	M50678	W50695

Class 120/1 (3 Cross Country) ■
Swindon Works, B.R.
Motor Brake Composite
Introduced: 1957
Engines:
Two B.U.T. (A.E.C.) 6-cyl. horizontal type of 150 b.h.p.
Body: 64′ 6″×9′ 3″
Weight: 36 tons (36 tons 7 cwt*)
Seats: **1st**, 18; **2nd**, 16
Works with Classes 120/2 and 179

M50696	W50712	W50728
M50697	M50713	W50729
W50698	M50714	M50730
W50699	W50715	M50731
W50700	W50716	W50732
W50701	M50717	W50733
W50702	M50718	M50734
M50703	M50719	W50735
M50704	M50720	M50736
W50705	W50721	M50737
W50706	W50722	W50738
W50707	W50723	W50739
M50708	W50724	M50741
M50709	M50725	M50742
W50710	W50726	M50743
W50711	W50727	M50744

Class 101/1 (3‡ or 4) ■
Metropolitan-Cammell
Motor Composite (L)
Introduced: 1957
For details see E50138

SC50746‡	SC50748	E50750
SC50747‡	SC50749	E50751

Class 105/2 (2† or 3) ■
Cravens
Motor Brake Second
Introduced: 1957
For details see E50249

M50752	M50762	M50771†
M50754	M50763	M50772†
M50755	M50764	M50773†
M50756	M50765	M50776†
M50757	E50766	M50777†
M50758	M50767	M50778†
M50759	M50768	M50779†
M50760	M50769	M50782†
M50761	M50770	M50784†

Class 105/1 († 105/3) (2* or 3)■

Cravens

Motor Composite (†Second) (L)

Introduced: 1957 (1958*)
Engines:
Two B.U.T. (A.E.C.) 6-cyl. horizontal type of 150 b.h.p.
Body: 57′ 6″×9′ 2″
Weight: 30 tons
Seats: 1st, 12; **2nd,** 51, **†2nd,** 63
Works with Class 105/2

M50785	M50794	M50804*
M50786†	M50795	M50805*
M50787	M50796	M50806*
M50788	M50797	M50807*
M50789	M50798	M50809*
M50790	M50800	M50810*
M50791	M50801	M50812*†
M50792	M50802	M50814*
M50793	M50803	M50815*

Class 116/2 (†130) (3 Suburban)■

Derby Works, B.R.

Motor Brake Second

Introduced: 1957
For details see M50050

SC50818	SC50836	M50854*
W50819†	M50837	W50855*R
SC50820	M50838	W50856*R
SC50821	SC50839	M50857*
SC50822	M50840	W50858*
SC50823	SC50841	M50859
E50824	W50842*R	M50860
SC50825	W50843*R	M50861
SC50826	E50844*	W50862†
E50827	E50845*	W50863*
E50828	SC50846	W50864*
SC50829	W50847*R	M50865*
E50830	W50848*	M50866*
M50831R	M50849	E50867
M50832R	M50850	W50868*
M50833R	W50851*	W50869*R
W50834*R	SC50852	M50870
M50835R	SC50853	

Class 116/1 (†130) (3 Suburban)■

Derby Works, B.R.

Motor Second

Introduced: 1957
For details see M50092

SC50871	M50890	M50907*
W50872†	M50891	W50908*R
SC50873	SC50892	W50909*R
SC50875	M50893	M50910*
SC50876	SC50894	W50911*
E50877	W50895*R	M50912
SC50878	W50896*R	M50913
SC50879	E50897*	M50914R
E50880	E50898*	W50915†*
SC50881	E50899	W50916*
SC50882	W50900*R	W50917*
E50883	W50901*	W50918*
M50884R	M50902	M50919*
M50885R	M50903	E50920
M50886	M50904*	M50921*
W50887R	SC50905	W50922*R
M50888R	E50906	M50923
SC50889		

Class 108/2 (2)■

Derby Works, B.R.

Motor Brake Second

Introduced: 1959
For details see E50599

M50924R	M50928	M50932
M50925	M50929	M50933
M50926	M50930	M50934R
M50927	M50931	M50935R

Class 126/1 (6 Inter-City)●

Swindon Works, B.R.

Motor Second (L)

Introduced: 1959
Engines:
Two B.U.T. (A.E.C.) 6-cyl. horizontal type of 150 b.h.p.
Body: 64′ 6″×9′ 3″. Gangwayed

both ends, side driving compartment at one end
Weight: 38 tons
Seats: 2nd, 64
Transmission:
Mechanical. Standard

SC50936

Class 108/2 (2)■

Derby Works, B.R.

Motor Brake Second

Introduced: 1959
For details see E50599

M50938	M50954	M50970
M50939	M50955	M50971
M50940	M50956	M50973
M50941	M50957	M50974
M50942	M50958	M50975
M50943R	M50959	M50976
M50944	M50960	M50977R
M50945R	M50962	M50978
M50947R	M50963	M50980
M50948	M50964	M50981R
M50949	M50965	M50982
M50950	M50966	M50983
M50951	M50967	M50985
M50952	M50968	M50986
M50953	M50969	M50987

Class 126/1 (6 Inter-City)●

Swindon Works, B.R.

Motor Second (L)

Introduced: 1959
For details see SC50936

SC51008	SC51016	SC51023
SC51009	SC51017	SC51024
SC51010	SC51018	SC51025
SC51012	SC51019	SC51026
SC51013	SC51020	SC51027
SC51014	SC51021	SC51029
SC51015	SC51022	

Class 126/2 (3 or 6 Inter-City)●

Swindon Works, B.R.

Motor Brake Second (L)

Introduced: 1959
Engines:
Two B.U.T. (A.E.C.) 6-cyl horizontal type of 150 b.h.p.
Body: 64′ 6″ × 9′ 3″. (Gangwayed at both ends, side driving compartment at one end*)
Weight: 38 tons
Seats: 2nd, 52
Transmission:
Mechanical. Standard

SC51030	SC51038	SC51045
SC51031	SC51039	SC51046
SC51032	SC51040	SC51047
SC51033	SC51041	SC51048
SC51034	SC51042	SC51049
SC51035	SC51043	SC51050
SC51036	SC51044	SC51051
SC51037		

Class 119/1 (3 Cross Country)■

Gloucester R. C. & W. Co.

Motor Brake Composite

Introduced: 1958
Engines:
Two B.U.T. (A.E.C.) (Leyland*) 6-cyl horizontal type of 150 b.h.p.
Body: 64′ 6″ × 9′ 3″
Weight: 37 tons
Seats: 1st, 18; **2nd,** 16
Works with Classes 119/2 and 178

W51052*	W51063*	M51072
W51054	W51064	M51073
W51055*	W51065*	M51074
W51056*	W51066*	W51075*
M51057	W51067*	M51076
M51058	W51068*	W51077*
M51059	W51069*	W51078*
W51060*	W51070*	W51079*
W51062*	M51071	

Class 119/2 motor second leads a Gloucester RCW 3-car cross-country unit at Lapford [G. F. Gillham

Class 119/2 (3 Cross Country) ■
Gloucester R. C. & W. Co.
Motor Second (L)

Introduced: 1958
Engines:
Two B.U.T. (A.E.C.) (Leyland*) 6-cyl horizontal type of 150 b.h.p.
Body: 64′ 6″ × 9′ 3″
Weight: 38 tons
Seats: 2nd, 68
Works with Classes 119/1 and 178

W51080*	W51091*	M51100
W51082	W51092	M51101
W51083*	W51093*	M51102
W51084*	W51094*	W51103*
M51085	W51095*	M51104
M51086	W51096*	W51105*
M51087	W51096*	W51106*
W51088*	W51097*	W51107*
W51090*	M51099	

Class 100 (2) ■
Gloucester R. C. & W. Co.
Motor Brake Second

Introduced: 1957
For details see M50340

M51110	M51117	E51124
M51112	M51119	E51126
E51115	E51120	E51127

Class 116/2 (3 Suburban)
Derby Works B.R.
Motor Brake Second

Introduced: 1958
For details see M50050

W51128R	W51132	M51136
M51129	M51133	M51138
M51130	W51134R	W51139R
M51131	W51135R	W51140*

Class 116/1 (3 Suburban) ■
Derby Works, B.R.
Motor Second

Introduced: 1958
For details see M50092

W51141R	W51145	M51149
M51142	M51146	M51151
M51143	W51147R	W51152R
M51144	W51148R	W51153*

Class 101/2 (2) ■
Metropolitan-Cammell
Motor Brake Second

Introduced: 1958
For details see E50152

M51174	M51201R	SC51227
M51175	M51202	SC51228
M51176	M51203	E51229
M51177	E51204	E51230R
M51178	E51205	SC51231
M51179R	E51206	SC51232
M51180	E51207	SC51233
M51181	E51208	SC51234
M51182R	E51209	SC51235
M51183R	E51210	E51236
M51184R	E51211	SC51237
M51185	E51212	SC51239
M51186	E51213	SC51240
M51187	E51214	SC51241
M51188	E51215	SC51242
M51189	E51216	SC51243
M51190	E51217	SC51244
M51191	E51218	SC51245
M51192	E51219	E51246
M51193	E51220R	E51247
M51194	E51221	SC51248
M51196	E51222	SC51249
M51197	E51223	SC51250
M51198	SC51224	SC51251
M51199	E51225	E51252
M51200R	E51226	SC51253

Class 105/2 (2)■
Cravens
Motor Brake Second
Introduced: 1958
For details see E50249

E51254	E51271	E51286
E51255	E51272	E51287
E51256	E51273	E51288
E51257	E51274	E51289
E51258	E51275	E51290
E51259	E51276	E51291
E51260	E51277	E51292
E51261	E51278	E51293
E51262	E51279	E51294
E51263	E51280	E51295
E51265	E51281	E51296
E51266	E51282	E51297
E51267	E51283	E51298
E51268	E51284	E51299
E51269	E51285	E51301
E51270		

Class 118/2 (3 Suburban)■
Birmingham R. C. & W. Co.
Motor Brake Second
Introduced: 1960
Engines:
Two B.U.T. (Leyland) 6-cyl horizontal type of 150 b.h.p.
Body: 64′ 0″×9′ 3″. Gangwayed, with side doors to each seating bay
Weight: 36 tons
Seats: 2nd, 65
Works with Classes 118/1 and 174

W51302	W51307	W51312
W51303	W51308	W51313
W51304	W51309	W51314
W51305	W51310	W51315
W51306	W51311	W51316

Class 118/1 (3 Suburban)■
Birmingham R. C. & W. Co.
Motor Second
Introduced: 1960
Engines:
Two B.U.T. (Leyland) 6-cyl horizontal type of 150 b.h.p.
Body: 64′ 0″×9′ 3″. Gangwayed, with side doors to each seating bay
Weight: 36 tons
Seats: 2nd, 89
Works with Classes 118/2 and 174

W51317	W51322	W51327
W51318	W51323	W51328
W51319	W51324	W51329
W51320	W51325	W51330
W51321	W51326	W51331

Class 117/2 (3 Suburban)■
Pressed Steel Co.
Motor Brake Second
Introduced: 1959
Engines:
Two B.U.T. (Leyland) 6-cyl. horizontal type of 150 b.h.p.
Body: 64′ 0″×9′ 3″. Gangwayed, with side doors to each seating bay
Weight: 36 tons
Seats: 2nd, 65
Works with Classes 117/1 and 176

W51332	W51346	W51361
W51333	W51347	W51362
W51334R	W51348R	W51363
W51335	W51349	W51364
W51336	W51350R	W51365
W51337R	W51351	W51366
W51338	W51352	W51367
W51339	W51353R	W51368
W51340	W51354	W51369
W51341	W51355	W51370
W51342	W51356	W51371
W51343	W51358	W51372
W51344	W51359	W51373
W51345R	W51360	

Swindon 3-car cross-country unit arriving at Bristol [*B. J. Nicolle*

Swindon 3-car inter-city unit on a Glasgow Central–Girvan working [*D. M. Cross*

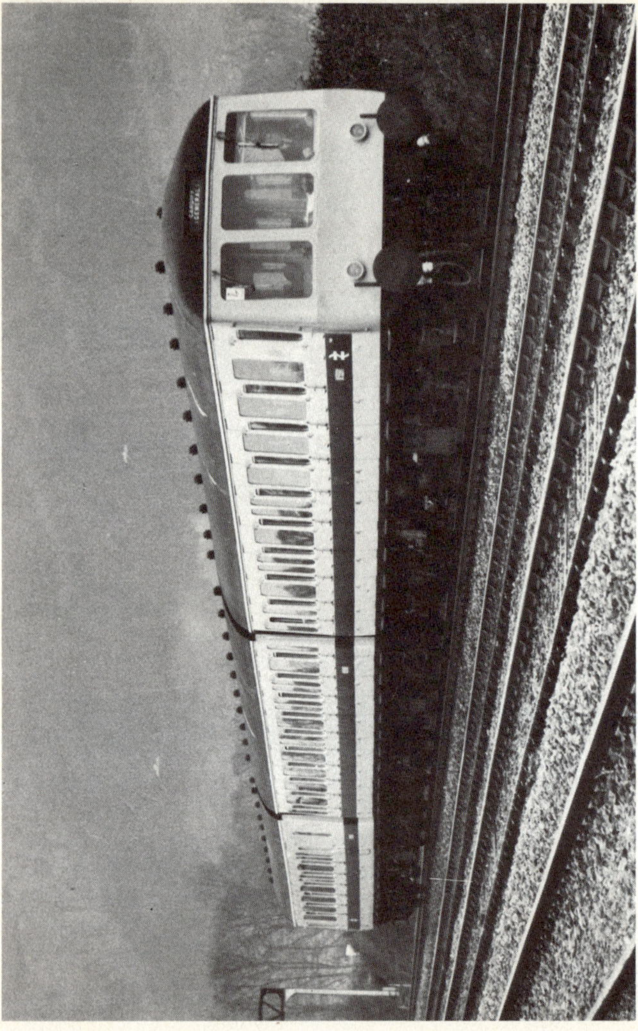

Refurbished Derby 3-car suburban unit on a Cardiff Valleys working

Class 117/1 (3 Suburban) ■

Pressed Steel Co.

Motor Second

Introduced: 1959

Engines:

Two B.U.T. (Leyland) 6-cyl. horizontal type of 150 b.h.p.

Body: 64′ 0″ × 9′ 3″. Ganwayed, with side doors to each seating bay

Weight: 36 tons

Seats: 2nd, 89

Works with Classes 117/2 and 176

W51374	W51388	W51402
W51375	W51389	W51403
W51376R	W51390R	W51404
W51377	W51391	W51405
W51378	W51392R	W51406
W51379R	W51393	W51407
W51380	W51394	W51408
W51381	W51395R	W51409
W51382	W51396	W51410
W51383	W51397	W51411
W51384	W51398	W51412
W51385	W51399	W51413
W51386	W51400	W51414
W51387R	W51401	W51415

Class 108/2 (2) ■

Derby Works, B.R.

Motor Brake Second

Introduced: 1960

For details see E50599

M51416	M51419	M51422
M51417	M51420	M51424
M51418	M51421	

Class 102/2 (2*, 3 or 4†) ■

Metropolitan-Cammell

Motor Brake Second

Introduced: 1959

Engines:

Two B.U.T. (Leyland) 6-cyl. horizontal type of 150 b.h.p.

Body: 57′ 0″ × 9′ 3″

Weight: 32 tons

Seats: 2nd, 52

Works with Classes 102/1, 162, 171, etc.

E51425*	E51440†	SC51456
E51426*R	E51441†	SC51457R
E51427*	E51442†R	SC51458R
E51428*	E51443†R	SC51459
E51429*	E51444R	SC51460
E51430*	W51445	SC51461R
E51431*	W51446	SC51462
E51432*	SC51448R	SC51463
E51433*	W51449	SC51464R
E51434*	W51450	SC51465R
E51435†	SC51451R	SC51466R
E51436†	W51452	SC51467R
E51437†R	SC51453R	SC51468
E51438†	SC51454R	SC51469
E51439†	SC51455	SC51470R

Class 105/2 (2) ■

Cravens

Motor Brake Second

Introduced: 1959

For details see E50249

E51471	SC51479	E51486
E51472	SC51480	E51487
SC51473	SC51481	E51489
SC51474	E51482	E51490
SC51475	SC51483	E51491
SC51476	E51484	E51492
SC51477	E51485	E51493
E51478		

Class 102/1 (2*, 3 or 4†) ■

Metropolitan-Cammell

Motor Composite (L)

Introduced: 1959

Engines:
Two B.U.T. (Leyland) 6-cyl. horizontal type of 150 b.h.p.
Body: 57′ 0″ × 9′ 3″
Weight: 32 tons
Seats: 1st, 12; **2nd,** 53
Works with Classes 102/2, 162, 171, etc.

E51495*	E51511†	SC51526R
E51496*	E51512†	SC51527R
E51497*	E51513†	SC51528R
E51498*	E51514†R	SC51529
E51499*	W51515	SC51530
E51500*	SC51516R	SC51531
E51501*	W51517	SC51532
E51502*	SC51518R	SC51533
E51503*	SC51519	SC51534
E51504*	SC51520	SC51535
E51505†	W51521	SC51536
E51506†R	W51522	SC51537
E51508†R	W51523	SC51538
E51509†	SC51524R	SC51539
E51510†	SC51525R	

Class 111/2 (3 or 2*) ■
Metropolitan-Cammell
Motor Brake Second
Introduced: 1959 (1960*)
For details see E50134

E51541	E51544	E51548*
E51542	E51545	E51549*
E51543	E51546	E51550*

Class 111/1 (3 or 2*) ■
Metropolitan-Cammell
Motor Composite (L)
Introduced: 1960
For details see E50270

E51551	E51555	E51558*
E51552	E51556	E51559*
E51553	E51557R	E51560*
E51554		

Class 108/1 (2) ■
Derby Works, B.R.
Motor Composite (L)
Introduced: 1959
For details see E50630

M51561†R	M51566†	M51570†R
M51562†	M51567†	M51571†R
M51563†	M51568†	M51572†R
M51565†	M51569†	

Class 120/1 (3 Cross Country) ■
Swindon Works, B.R.
Motor Brake Composite (L)
Introduced: 1961
For details see M50696

W51573*	W51576*	W51579*
W51574*	W51577*	W51580*
W51575*	W51578*	W51581*

Class 120/2 (3 Cross Country) ■
Swindon Works, B.R.
Motor Second (L)
Introduced: 1961
For details see W50647

W51582	W51585	W51588
W51583	W51586	W51589
W51584	W51587	W51590

Class 127 (4 Suburban) ▲
Derby Works, B.R.
Motor Brake Second
Introduced: 1959
Engines:
Two Rolls-Royce 8-cyl horizontal type of 238 b.h.p.
Transmission:
Hydraulic. Torque converter
Body: 64′ 0″ × 9′ 3″. Non-gangwayed, side doors to each seating bay
Weight: 40 tons
Seats: 2nd, 78

Birmingham RCW 3-car unit with Class 118/1 motor second leading [*B. J. Nicolle*

Derby 3-car suburban unit with Class 116/2 motor brake second leading [*B. J. Nicolle*

M51592	M51613	M51633
M51593	M51614	M51634
M51595	M51615	M51635
M51596	M51616	M51636
M51597	M51617	M51637
M51598	M51618	M51638
M51599	M51619	M51639
M51600	M51620	M51640
M51601	M51621	M51641
M51603	M51622	M51642
M51604	M51623	M51643
M51605	M51624	M51644
M51606	M51625	M51645
M51607	M51626	M51646
M51608	M51627	M51647
M51610	M51628	M51648
M51611	M51630	M51649
M51612	M51631	M51650

Class 115 **(4** Suburban**)** ■

Derby Works, B.R.

Motor Brake Second

Introduced: 1960

Engines:

Two B.U.T. (Leyland Albion) 6-cyl horizontal type of 230 b.h.p.

Body: 64′ 0″ × 9′ 3″. Non-gangwayed, side doors to each seating bay

Weight: 38 tons

Seats: 2nd, 78

Works with Class 186

M51651	M51661	M51671
M51652	M51662	M51672
M51653	M51663	M51673
M51654	M51664	M51674
M51655	M51665	M51675
M51656	M51666	M51676
M51657	M51667	M51677
M51658	M51668	M51678
M51659	M51669	M51679
M51660	M51670	M51680

Class 120/1 (3 Cross Country**)** ■

Swindon Works, B.R.

Motor Brake Composite

Introduced: 1959

For details see M50696

SC51781*	SC51784*	SC51786*
SC51782*	SC51785*	SC51787*
SC51783*R		

Class 120/2 (3 Cross Country**)** ■

Swindon Works, B.R.

Motor Second (L)

Introduced: 1960

For details see W50647

SC51788	SC51791	SC51793
SC51789	SC51792R	SC51794
SC51790		

Class 102/2 **(3)** ■

Metropolitan-Cammell

Motor Brake Second

Introduced: 1959

For details see E51425

SC51795	SC51798	SC51800
SC51796	SC51799	SC51801
SC51797		

Class 102/1 **(3)** ■

Metropolitan-Cammell

Motor Composite (L)

Introduced: 1959

For details see E51495

SC51802R	SC51805	SC51807R
SC51803	SC51806R	SC51808
SC51804R		

Pressed Steel Class 117/2 motor brake second No. W51345 [*B. J. Nicolle*

Swindon 3-car cross-country unit [*B. J. Nicolle*

Class 110/2 (3)■
Birmingham R. C. & W. Co.
Motor Brake Composite
Introduced: 1961
Engines:
Two Rolls-Royce Series 130D of 180 b.h.p.
Body: 57′ 6″×9′ 3″
Weight: 32 tons
Seats: 1st, 12; **2nd**, 33
Works with Classes 110/1 and 163

E51809	E51816	E51823
E51810	E51817	E51824
E51811	E51818	E51825
E51812	E51819	E51826
E51813	E51820	E51827
E51814	E51822	E51828
E51815		

Class 110/1 (3)■
Birmingham R. C. & W. Co.
Motor Composite (L)
Introduced: 1961
Engines:
Two Rolls-Royce Series 130D of 180 b.h.p.
Body: 57′ 6″×9′ 3″
Weight: 31 tons 10 cwt
Seats: 1st, 12; **2nd**, 54
Works with Classes 110/2 and 163

E51829	E51836	E51843
E51830	E51838	E51844
E51831	E51839	E51845
E51832	E51840	E51846
E51833	E51841	E51847
E51834	E51842	E51848
E51835		

Class 115 (**4** Suburban)■
Derby Works, B.R.
Motor Brake Second
Introduced: 1960
For details see M51651

M51849	M51867	M51884
M51850	M51868	M51885
M51851	M51869	M51886
M51852	M51870	M51887
M51853	M51871	M51888
M51854	M51872	M51889
M51855	M51873	M51890
M51856	M51874	M51891
M51857	M51875	M51892
M51858	M51876	M51893
M51859	M51877	M51894
M51860	M51878	M51895
M51861	M51879	M51896
M51862	M51880	M51897
M51863	M51881	M51898
M51864	M51882	M51899
M51865	M51883	M51900
M51866		

Class 108/2 (2)■
Derby Works, B.R.
Motor Brake Second
Introduced: 1960
For details see E50599

M51901	M51917	M51933
M51902R	M51918	M51934
M51903R	M51919	M51935
M51904R	M51920	M51936
M51905	M51922	M51937R
M51906	M51923	M51938
M51907	M51924	M51939
M51908	M51925R	M51940
M51909	M51926	M51941
M51910	M51927	M51942
M51911	M51928	M51943
M51912	M51929R	M51945
M51913	M51930	M51947
M51914	M51931R	M51948
M51916	M51932	M51950

Class 124/1 (**5** Trans-Pennine)■
Swindon Works, B.R.
Motor Composite
Introduced: 1960

Metro-Cammell Class 102/1 motor composite No. SC51527 [*B. J. Nicolle*

Derby 4-car suburban unit on a Bedford–St. Pancras working [*B. Morrison*

Swindon Trans-Pennine unit (reduced to 5 cars)

[*L. Goddard*

Engines:
Two B.U.T. (Leyland Albion) 6-cyl horizontal type of 230 b.h.p.
Body: 64′ 6″×9′ 3″
Weight: 40 tons
Seats: 1st, 21; **2nd**, 36
Works with Classes 124/2 and 180

E51951	E51957	E51963
E51952	E51958	E51964
E51953	E51960	E51965
E51954	E51961	E51966
E51955	E51962	E51967
E51956		

Class 124/2
(5 Trans-Pennine**)** ■
Swindon Works, B.R.
Motor Brake Second (K)
(non-driving)
Introduced: 1960
Engines:
Two B.U.T.(Leyland Albion) 6-cyl horizontal type of 230 b.h.p.
Body: 64′ 6″×9′ 3″
Weight: 41 tons
Seats: 2nd, 48
Works with Classes 124/1 and 180

E51968	E51974	E51980
E51969	E51975	E51981
E51970	E51976	E51982
E51971	E51977	E51983
E51972	E51978	E51984
E51973	E51979	

Class 107/2 (3) ■
Derby Works, B.R.
Motor Brake Second
Introduced: 1960
Engines:
Two B.U.T. (A.E.C.) 6-cyl horizontal type of 150 b.h.p.
Body: 58′ 1″×9′ 3″
Weight: 34 tons 10 cwt
Seats: 2nd, 52
Works with Classes 107/1 and 161

SC51985	SC51994	SC52003
SC51986	SC51996	SC52004
SC51987	SC51997	SC52005
SC51988	SC51998	SC52006
SC51989	SC51999	SC52007
SC51990	SC52000	SC52008
SC51991	SC52001	SC52009
SC51992	SC52002	SC52010
SC51993		

Class 107/1 (3) ■
Derby Works, B.R.
Motor Composite (L)
Introduced: 1960
Engines:
Two B.U.T. (A.E.C.) 6-cyl horizontal type of 150 b.h.p.
Body: 58′ 1″×9′ 3″
Weight: 35 tons
Seats: 1st, 12; **2nd**, 53
Works with Classes 107/2 and 161

SC52011	SC52020	SC52029
SC52012	SC52021	SC52030
SC52013	SC52022	SC52031
SC52014	SC52023	SC52032
SC52015	SC52024	SC52033
SC52016	SC52025	SC52034
SC52017	SC52026	SC52035
SC52018	SC52027	SC52036
SC52019	SC52028	

Class 108/1 (2) ■
Derby Works, B.R.
Motor Composite (L)
Introduced: 1960
For details see E50630

M52037‡R	M52043‡R	M52049‡
M52038‡	M52044‡	M52050‡
M52039‡R	M52045‡	M52051‡
M52040‡	M52046‡	M52052‡
M52041‡	M52047‡	M52053‡
M52042‡R	M52048‡	M52054‡

Swindon 3- and 4-car inter-city units at Colthrop [*D. E. Canning*

M52055‡	M52059‡	M52063‡
M52056‡	M52060‡	M52064‡R
M52057‡	M52061‡	M52065‡
M52058‡	M52062‡	

Class 110/2 (3)■
Birmingham R.C. & W. Co.
Motor Brake Composite
Introduced: 1961
For details see E51809

E52066	E52069	E52072
E52067	E52070	E52073
E52068	E52071	E52075

Class 110/1 (3)■
Birmingham R. C. & W. Co.
Motor Composite (L)
Introduced: 1961
For details see E51829

E52076	E52080	E52083
E52077	E52081	E52084
E52078	E52082	E52085
E52079		

Class 123/2
(**3 or 4** Inter-City)■
Swindon Works, B.R.
Motor Brake Second (L)
Introduced: 1963
Engines:
Two B.U.T. (Leyland Albion) 6-cyl. horizontal type of 230 b.h.p.
Body: 64′ $11\frac{1}{8}$″ × 9′ 3″
Weight: 41 tons 14 cwt
Seats: 2nd, 32
Works with Classes 123/1 and 182, 183

W52086	W52090	E52093
W52087	E52091	W52094
W52088	E52092	W52095
W52089		

Class 123/1
(**3 or 4** Inter-City)■
Swindon Works, B.R.
Motor Second (K)
Introduced: 1963
Engines:
Two B.U.T. (Leyland Albion) 6-cyl. horizontal type of 230 b.h.p.
Body: 64′ $11\frac{1}{8}$″ × 9′ 3″
Weight: 41 tons 9 cwt
Seats: 2nd, 56
Works with Classes 123/2 and 182, 183

W52096	W52099	W52103
E52097	W52100	W52104
E52098	W52102	E52105

Class 122 (*131) (1)■
Gloucester R. C. & W. Co.
Motor Brake Second
Introduced: 1958
Engines:
Two B.U.T. (A.E.C.) 6-cyl. horizontal type of 150 b.h.p.
Body: 64′ 6″ × 9′ 3″. Non-gangwayed, side doors to each seating bay (*converted for parcels traffic)
Weight: 36 tons
Seats: 2nd, 65
Single-car or works with Class 150

SC55000	M55006	M55012
SC55002	SC55007	SC55013*
M55003	M55009	SC55014*
M55004	SC55011	SC55015*
SC55005		

Class 121 (1)■
Pressed Steel Co.
Motor Brake Second
Introduced: 1960

Engines:
Two B.U.T. (A.E.C.) (Leyland*) 6-cyl. horizontal type of 150 b.h.p.
Body: 64′ 6″×9′ 3″. Non-gangwayed, side doors to each seating bay
Weight: 37 tons 8 cwt
Seats: 2nd, 65
Single car or works with Class 149

W55020*	W55026*	W55031
W55021	W55027	W55032
W55022	W55028	W55033
W55023*	W55029*	W55034
W55024*	W55030*	W55035
W55025		

Class 128 (1)■
Gloucester R. C. & W. Co.
Motor Parcels Van

Introduced: 1959
Engines:
Two B.U.T. (Leyland Albion) 6-cyl. horizontal type of 230 b.h.p.
Body: 64′ 6″×9′ 3″ (Non-gangwayed*)
Weight: 41 tons (40 tons*)
Single car can haul a tail load. Works with Class 130

M55988*	W55991	M55994
M55989*	W55992	M55995
M55990*	M55993	M55996

Class 148 (2)■
Derby Works, B.R.
Driving Trailer Composite (L)

Introduced: 1956
Body: 64′ 6″×9′ 3″
Weight: 29 tons 10 cwt
Seats: 1st, 12; **2nd,** 62
Works with Class 114

E56001	E56006	E56011
E56002	E56007	E56012
E56003	E56008	E56013
E56004	E56009	E56014
E56005	E56010	E56015

E56016	E56027	E56038
E56017	E56028	E56039
E56018R	E56029	E56040
E56019	E56030	E56041
E56021	E56032	E56042
E56022	E56033	E56043
E56023	E56034	E56044
E56024	E56035	E56045
E56025	E56036	E56047
E56026	E56037	E56049

Class 144 (*147) (2)■
Metropolitan-Cammell
Driving Trailer Composite (‡Second) (L)

Introduced: 1957
Body: 57′ 0″×9′ 3″
Weight: 25 tons
Seats: 1st, 12; **2nd,** 53, (45†), ‡**2nd,** 65

E56050	E56065	E56080
E56051	E56066	E56081
E56052	E56067R	E56082
E56053	E56068R	E56083
E56054	E56069	E56084
M56055	E56070R	E56085
E56056	E56071	E56086
E56057	E56072	E56087
M56058‡	E56073R	E56088R
E56059	E56074	E56089
M56060R	E56075R	E56090*R
E56061	E56076	E56091*
E56062	E56077	E56092*
E56063R	E56078	E56093*
E56064R	E56079	

Class 143 (2)■
Gloucester R. C. & W. Co.
Driving Trailer Composite (*Second) (L)

Introduced: 1957
Body: 57′ 6″×9′ 3″
Weight: 25 tons
Seats: 1st, 12; **2nd,** 54, ***2nd,** 66

E56100	M56104*	M56106*
M56103*	M56105*	M56107*

Gloucester Class 122 single unit No. W55016 at Looe [*R. Barton*

Gloucester RCW Class 128 motor parcels van No. M55988 [*B. Morrison*

Pressed Steel Class 121 single unit No. W55033 [*B. J. Nicolle*

M56108*	M56110*	M56112*
M56109*	M56111*	M56113*

Class 141 (2)■
Cravens

Driving Trailer Composite (*Second) (L)

Introduced: 1956
Body: 57′ 6″ × 9′ 2″
Weight: 23 tons (24 tons†)
Seats: 1st, 12; **2nd**, 51, ***2nd**, 63

E56114	M56127	E56138
E56115*	E56128	E56139*
E56116	M56129	E56140
M56118	E56130	E56141
E56119	E56131*	E56142
M56120	E56132*	E56143
E56121	E56133	E56144
E56122	E56134	M56145
E56123	E56135	M56146
E56124	E56136	M56148
E56125	E56137	M56149
E56126		

Class 145 (2)■
Park Royal Vehicles

Driving Trailer Composite (L)

Introduced: 1957
Body: 57′ 6″ × 9′ 3″
Weight: 26 tons 10 cwt
Seats: 1st, 16; **2nd**, 48

M56150	M56156	M56161
M56151	M56157	M56163
M56152	M56158	M56164
M56155	M56159	M56165

Class 140 (2)■
Birmingham R. C. & W. Co.

Driving Trailer Second (*Composite) (L)

Introduced: 1958
Body: 57′ 6″ × 9′ 3″
Weight: 24 tons
Seats: 2nd, 66
***1st**, 12; **2nd**, 54

M56175	M56180	E56185*
M56176	M56181	E56186*
M56177	M56182	E56187*
M56178	M56183	E56188*
M56179	M56184	E56189*

Class 142 (2)■
Derby Works, B.R.

Driving Trailer Composite (L)

Introduced: 1958
Body: 57′ 6″ × 9′ 2″
Weight: 21 tons (22 tons*)
Seats: 1st, 12; **2nd**, 53
†**2nd**, 65
Works with Class 108/2

E56190	E56198R	E56207
E56191R	E56199R	E56208R
E56192R	E56200R	E56209R
E56193	E56201	E56210R
E56194R	E56202R	M56212
E56195R	E56203R	M56213
E56196R	E56204R	M56214
E56197R	E56205R	

Class 144 (2)■
Metropolitan-Cammell

Driving Trailer Composite (L)

Introduced: 1957
For details see E56050

E56218†	E56219†	E56220†

Class 142 (2)■
Derby Works, B.R.

Driving Trailer Composite (†Second) (L)

Introduced: 1959
For details see E56190

M56221	M56230R	M56238
M56222	M56231	M56239
M56223	M56232	M56240
M56224	M56233	M56241
M56225	M56234	M56242
M56227	M56235	M56243
M56228R	M56236	M56244

Park Royal 2-car unit (now preserved) passing Shiplake [*C. J. Leigh*

M56245	M56258	M56269
M56246	M56259	M56270
M56247	M56260R	M56271*
M56248	M56261	M56272*
M56249	M56262	M56273*
M56250	M56263	M56274*
M56251	M56264	M56275*
M56252	M56265	M56276*
M56253R	M56266	M56277*
M56256	M56267†	M56278*
M56257	M56268	M56279*

Class 149 (2)■
Pressed Steel Co.

Driving Trailer Second

For use with Class 121 and 122 Single Unit cars

Introduced: 1960

Body: 64′ 0″ × 9′ 3″. Non-gangwayed, side doors to each seating bay

Weight: 29 tons 7 cwt

Seats: 2nd, 91

W56280	W56284	W56287
W56281	W56285	W56289
W56283	W56286	

Class 150 ■
Gloucester R. C. & W. Co.

Driving Trailer Second

For use with Class 121 and 122 Single Unit cars

Introduced: 1958

Body: 64′ 0″ × 9′ 3″. Non-gangwayed, side doors to each seating bay

Weight: 27 tons

Seats: 2nd, 91

M56295 M56296

Class 143 (2)■
Gloucester R. C. & W. Co.

Driving Trailer Composite (L)

Introduced: 1957

For details see E56100

E56307 E56316

Class 144 (2)■
Metropolitan-Cammell

Driving Trailer Composite (‡ Second) (L)

Introduced: 1958

For details see E56050

M56332	M56359	E56385R
M56333R	M56360	SC56386
M56334	M56361	E56387
M56335	E56362	SC56388
M56336	E56363	SC56389
M56337	E56364	SC56390
M56339R	E56365	SC56391
M56340	E56366	E56392
M56341R	E56367	E56393
M56342R	E56368	E56394R
M56343	E56369R	E56396
M56344R	E56370	E56397
M56345	E56371	E56398
M56346	E56372R	E56399
M56347	E56373R	E56400
M56348R	E56374	E56401R
M56349	E56375	E56402R
M56350	E56376	SC56403
M56351R	E56377	SC56404
M56352	E56378	E56405
M56353	E56379	SC56406
M56354	E56380	SC56407
M56355	E56381	SC56408
M56356	E56382R	E56409
M56357	E56383R	E56410
M56358	E56384	M56411‡

Class 141 (2)■
Cravens

Driving Trailer Composite (*Second) (L)

Introduced: 1958

For details see E56114

Two Cravens 2-car units led by Class 105/2 motor brake second [B. J. Nicolle

E56413*†	E56436†	E56459*†
E56414*†	E56437†	E56460*
E56415*†	E56438*†	E56461*
E56416*†	E56439†	E56462
E56417*†	E56440†	E56463
E56418*†	E56441†	E56464
E56419*†	E56442†	E56465
E56420*†	E56443†	E56466
E56421*†	E56444†	E56467
E56422*†	E56445†	E56468
E56423*†	E56446†	E56469
E56424*†	E56447*†	E56470
E56425*†	E56448*†	E56471
E56426*†	E56449*†	E56472
E56427*†	E56450*†	E56473
E56428*†	E56451*†	E56474
E56429*†	M56452*†	M56475
E56430*†	E56453*†	E56476
E56431*†	E56454*†	E56477
E56432*†	E56455*†	E56478
E56433*†	M56456*†	E56479
E56434†	E56457*†	E56480
E56435†	E56458*†	M56482

Class 142 (2) ■

Derby Works, B.R.

Driving Trailer Composite (L)

Introduced: 1960

For details see E56190

M56484*	M56491*	M56498*
M56485*R	M56492*	M56499*
M56486*R	M56493*	M56500*
M56487*R	M56494*	M56501*R
M56488*	M56495*	M56502*
M56489*	M56496*	M56503*
M56490*	M56497*	M56504*

Class 175 (3 Suburban) ■

Derby Works, B.R.

Trailer Composite (†Second)

Introduced: 1957

Body: 63′ 8¾″×9′ 3″. Non-gangwayed (*gangwayed), with side doors to each seating bay

Weight: 28 tons 10 cwt

Seats: 1st, 28; **2nd,** 74; †**2nd,** 102

M59000†R	M59011†	M59021†
M59001†R	M59012†R	M59022†
M59002†	M59013†R	M59023†
M59003†R	M59014†	M59024†
M59004†	M59015†	M59026†R
M59005†R	M59016†	M59027†
M59006†	M59017†	M59028†
M59007†	M59018†	M59029†R
M59008†	M59019†R	W59030*R
M59009†R	M59020†	W59031*R
M59010†		

Class 172 (3 Suburban) ■

Derby Works, B.R.

Trailer Second

Introduced: 1957

Body: 63′ 8¾″ × 9′ 3″. Non-gangwayed (*gangwayed), with side doors to each seating bay

Weight: 29 tons

Seats: 2nd, 106

W59032*	W59036R	W59039*R
W59033R	W59037R	W59040*R
W59034	W59038R	W59041
W59035R		

Class 162 (4) ■

Metropolitan-Cammell

Trailer Second (L)

Introduced: 1956

Body: 57′ 0″×9′ 3″

Weight: 25 tons

Seats: 2nd, 61 (71*)

E59042	E59045	E59047
SC59043	E59046	E59048

Class 168 (4) ■

Metropolitan-Cammell

Trailer Brake Second (L)

Introduced: 1956

Body: 57′ 0″×9′ 3″

A mixed rake of dmu vehicles near Ruabon with a Park Royal motor brake second leading

Weight: 25 tons
Seats: **2nd**, 45 (53*)

E59049	E59052	E59054R
E59050	SC59053	E59055R

Class 162 (4) ■
Metropolitan-Cammell
Trailer Second (L)
Introduced: 1957
For details see E59042

SC59060*	E59065*R	SC59069*
SC59061*	SC59066*	E59070*R
E59062*R	SC59067*	E59071*
E59063*	E59068*	E59072*
E59064*		

Class 168 (4) ■
Metropolitan-Cammell
Trailer Brake Second (L)
Introduced: 1957
For details see E59049

E59073*	E59078*	E59082*
SC59074*	E59079*	E59083*
E59075*R	SC59080*	E59084*R
E59076*	M59081*	E59085*
E59077*		

Class 162 (4) ■
Metropolitan-Cammell
Trailer Second (L)
Introduced: 1957
For details see E59042

E59086	SC59088	E59090
E59087R	E59089R	E59091

Class 168 (4) ■
Metropolitan-Cammell
Trailer Brake Second (L)
Introduced: 1957
For details see E59049

E59092	E59094R	E59096
E59093	E59095	E59097

Class 164 (3) ■
Metropolitan-Cammell
Trailer Second (L)
Introduced: 1957
Body: 57′ 0″ × 9′ 3″
Weight: 25 tons
Seats: **2nd**, 71

E59100	E59104	E59107
E59101	E59105	E59108
E59102	E59106	SC59109

Class 168 (4) ■
Metropolitan-Cammell
Trailer Brake Second (L)
Introduced: 1957
For details see E59049

SC59112* E59113*

Class 171 (3) ■
Metropolitan-Cammell
Trailer Composite (*Second) (L)
Introduced: 1958
Body: 57′ 0″ × 9′ 3″
Weight: 25 tons
Seats: **1st**, 12; **2nd**, 53

M59114*	M59120*	M59126*
M59115*R	M59121*	M59127*
M59116*	M59122*	M59128*
M59117*	M59123*R	M59129*
M59118*	M59124*R	M59130
M59119*R	M59125*	M59131

Class 169 (3) ■
Birmingham R. C. & W. Co.
Trailer Composite (*Second) (L)

Metro-Cammell 3-car unit refurbished in Greater Glasgow PTE livery [*GGPTE*

Introduced: 1957
Body: 57′ 0″ × 9′ 3″
Weight: 24 tons
Seats: 1st, 12; **2nd,** 54
***2nd,** 66

M59132*	M59150	M59171
M59133*	M59151	M59172
M59134*	M59152	M59173
M59135*	M59153	M59174
M59136*	M59155	M59175
M59137*	M59156	M59176
M59138*	M59157	M59177
M59139*	M59158	M59178
M59140*	M59159	M59179
M59141*	M59160	M59180
M59142	M59161	M59181
M59143	M59162	M59182
M59144	M59163	M59183
M59145*	M59164	M59184
M59146	M59165	M59185
M59147*	M59166	M59186
M59148*	M59168	M59187
M59149	M59169	

Class 160 (4) ■
Birmingham R. C. & W. Co.
Trailer Second (L)

Introduced: 1958
Body: 57′ 0″ × 9′ 3″
Weight: 24 tons
Seats: 2nd, 69

E59188	E59194	E59201
E59189	M59195	E59203
E59190	E59197	E59204
E59191	M59198	E59206
E59192	E59199	E59207
E59193	E59200	E59208

Class 166 (4) ■
Birmingham R. C. & W. Co.
Trailer Brake Second (L)

Introduced: 1958
Body: 57′ 0″ × 9′3″
Weight: 25 tons
Seats: 2nd, 51

E59209	E59210	E59211
E59212	E59218	E59225
E59213	E59219	E59226
E59214	E59220	E59227
E59215	E59221	E59228
E59216	E59223	E59229
E59217	E59224	

Class 160 (4) ■
Birmingham R. C. & W. Co.
Trailer Second (L)

Introduced: 1958
For details see E59188

M59230	E59232	E59234
E59231	E59233	

Class 182 (3 or 4 Inter-City) ■
Swindon Works, B.R.
Trailer Second (L)

Introduced: 1963
Body: 64′ 6″ × 9′ 3″
Weight: 31 tons 9 cwt
Seats: 2nd, 64

E59235	E59237	E59239
E59236	E59238	

Class 166 (4) ■
Birmingham R.C. & W. Co.
Trailer Brake Second (L)

Introduced: 1958
For details see E59209

E59240	E59242	E59244
E59241	E59243	

Class 167 (4) ■
Derby Works, B.R.
Trailer Brake Second (L)

Introduced: 1958
Body: 57′ 6″ × 9′ 2″
Weight: 23 tons
Seats: 2nd, 50

E59245R	E59247R	E59249R
E59246R	E59248	E59250R

THE SMOKEBOX

AT

3 QUEBEC HOUSE
CROMWELL ROAD
KINGSTON UPON
THAMES
SURREY KT2 6RF
01-549 9700

BRITAIN'S NEWEST
BOOKSHOP FOR RAIL AND BUS
FANS WELCOMES YOU

ONLY 45 MINS. FROM THE
CENTRE OF LONDON!

BOOKS · RELICS · PERIODICALS · ETC.

BOUGHT–SOLD–PART EXCHANGED

OPEN TUESDAY–SATURDAY 10 TILL 6

Class 179 (3 Cross Country) ■
Swindon Works, B.R.
Trailer Buffet Second (L)

Introduced: 1958
Body: 64′ 6″×9′ 3″. Open second with miniature buffet at one end
Weight: 31 tons (30 tons 12 cwt*)
Seats: 2nd, 60; **Buffet**, 4
Works with Classes 120/1 and 120/2

M59255	M59272	M59287
M59256	M59273	W59288
M59257	M59274	M59289
M59258	W59275	M59290
M59259	M59276	W59291
W59260	W59277	W59292
W59261	W59278	M59293
W59262	W59279	W59294
M59263	M59280	M59295
W59264	M59281	W59296
W59265	W59282	M59297
W59266	M59283	W59299
M59267	W59284	M59300
W59268	W59285	M59301
W59269	W59286	

Class 162 (3 or 4†) ■
Metropolitan-Cammell
Trailer Second (L)

Introduced: 1957
For details see E59040

SC59302*	SC59304*	E59306*†R
SC59303*	SC59305*	

Class 175 (3 Suburban) ■
Derby Works, B.R.
Trailer Composite (†Second)

Introduced: 1957
For details see M59000

SC59326	M59334†R	M59341†R
SC59328	E59335*	M59342†
SC59329	E59336	E59343
SC59330	SC59337	SC59344
SC59331	M59338†	SC59345
E59332	M59339†R	M59346*†
SC59333	W59340*R	SC59347
M59348†	M59358†	SC59367
SC59349	W59359*	M59368*†
W59350*R	SC59360	W59369*
M59351†	E59361	W59371*
M59352*†	W59362*	M59372*†
E59353*	W59363*R	W59373*
SC59354	W59364*R	M59374*
W59355*R	W59365*	E59375
W59356*	W59366*	M59376†
W59357*R		

Class 161 (3 or 4*) ■
Derby Works, B.R.
Trailer Second (L)

Introduced: 1958
Body: 58′ 1″×9′ 3″
*†57′ 6″×9′ 2″
Weight: 28 tons (22 tons*, 22 tons 10 cwt†)
Seats: **2nd**, 71 (68*†)

E59380*	E59384*	E59388†
E59381*R	E59385*	E59389†R
E59382*R	E59386†	E59390†R
E59383*	E59387†R	

Class 189 (3 or 6 Inter-City) ●
Swindon Works, B.R.
Trailer First (K)

Introduced: 1959
Body: 64′ 6″×9′ 3″
Weight: 33 tons 8 cwt
Seats: **1st**, 42

SC59391	SC59395	SC59398
SC59392	SC59396	SC59399
SC59393	SC59397	SC59400
SC59394		

Class 189 (3 or 6 Inter-City) ●
Swindon Works B.R.
Trailer Composite (L)

Introduced: 1959
Body: 64′ 6″×9′ 3″

Weight: 31 tons 16 cwt
Seats: **1st**, 18; **2nd**, 32

SC59402	SC59406	SC59410
SC59403	SC59407	SC59411
SC59404	SC59408	SC59412
SC59405	SC59409	

Class 178 (3 Cross Country) ■
Gloucester R. C. & W. Co.
Trailer Buffet Second (L)

Introduced: 1958
Body: 64′ 6″×9′ 3″. Open second with miniature buffet at one end
Weight: 31 tons
Seats: **2nd**, 60; **Buffet**, 4
Works with Classes 119/1 and 119/2

W59413	W59422	M59430
M59414	W59423	M59431
W59415	W59424	M59432
M59416	W59425	M59433
W59417	W59426	W59434
M59418	W59427	M59435
W59419	W59428	W59436
W59420	W59429	W59437
W59421		

Class 175 (3 Suburban) ■
Derby Works, B.R.
Trailer Composite (†Second)

Introduced: 1958
For details see M59000

M59438†	M59442†R	W59445R
M59439†	M59443†	W59446
M59440†	W59444*R	M59448†
M59441†		

Class 174 (3 Suburban) ■
Birmingham R. C. & W. Co.
Trailer Composite (L)

Introduced: 1960
Body: 63′ 10″×9′ 3″. Gangwayed, with side doors to each seating bay
Weight: 30 tons
Seats: **1st**, 22; **2nd**, 48
Works with Classes 118/1 and 118/2

W59469	W59474	W59479
W59470	W59475	W59480
W59471	W59476	W59481
W59472	W59477	W59482
W59473	W59478	W59483

Class 176 (3 Suburban) ■
Pressed Steel Co.
Trailer Composite (L)

Introduced: 1959
Body: 63′ 10″ × 9′ 3″. Gangwayed, with side doors to each seating bay
Weight: 30 tons
Seats: **1st**, 22; **2nd**, 48
Works with Classes 117/1 and 117/2

W59484	W59497R	W59510
W59485	W59498	W59511
M59486	W59499	W59512
W59487	W59500	W59513
W59488	W59501	W59514
W59489R	W59502R	W59515
W59490	W59503	W59516
W59491	W59504	W59517
W59492	W59505R	W59518
W59493	W59506	W59519
W59494	W59507	W59520
W59495	W59508	W59521
W59496	W59509	W59522

Class 171 (3 or 4*) ■
Metropolitan-Cammell
Trailer Composite (L)

Introduced: 1959
For details see M59114

E59523*R	E59527*	E59531*
E59524*R	M59528*	E59532*
E59525*	E59529*	E59533*
E59526*	E59530*	E59534*

E59535*	W59547	SC59558R
E59536*	SC59548	SC59559
W59538*	W59549	SC59560
SC59539*	W59550	SC59561
E59540*	W59551	SC59562R
SC59541*	SC59552R	SC59563R
E59542*	SC59553R	SC59564
W59543	SC59554	SC59565R
SC59544	SC59555	SC59566
SC59545R	SC59556R	SC59567
W59546	SC59557	SC59568R

Class 164 (3) ■

Metropolitan-Cammell

Trailer Second (L)

Introduced: 1959
For details see E59100

E59569R	E59571	E59572
E59570		

Class 165 (4) ■

Metropolitan-Cammell

Trailer Buffet Second (L)

Introduced: 1960
Body: 57′ 0″×9′ 3″ Open second with miniature buffet at one end
Weight: 25 tons
Seats: 2nd, 53

E59574	E59577	E59578

Class 179 (3 Cross Country) ■

Swindon Works, B.R.

Trailer Buffet Second (L)

Introduced: 1960
For details see M59255

W59580*	W59583*	W59587*
W59581*	W59586*	W59588*
W59582*		

Class 186 (4 Suburban) ▲

Derby Works, B.R.

Trailer Second (L*)

Introduced: 1959
Body: 63′ 10″ × 9′ 3″ (63′ 8¾″ × 9′ 3″*). Non-gangwayed, side doors to each seating bay. (Intermediate lavatories on each side of central passageway*)
Weight: 29 tons (30 tons*)
Seats: 2nd, 106 (90*)

M59589*	M59609*	M59629
M59590*	M59610*	M59631
M59591*	M59611*	M59632
M59592*	M59612*	M59633
M59593*	M59613*	M59634
M59594*	M59614*	M59636
M59595*	M59615*	M59637
M59596*	M59616*	M59638
M59597*	M59617*	M59639
M59598*	M59619	M59640
M59600*	M59620	M59641
M59602*	M59621	M59642
M59603*	M59622	M59643
M59604*	M59623	M59644
M59605*	M59625	M59645
M59606*	M59626	M59646
M59607*	M59627	M59647
M59608*	M59628	M59648

Class 173 (4 Suburban) ■

Derby Works, B.R.

Trailer Second

Introduced: 1960
Body: 63′ 8¾″ × 9′ 3″. Non-gangwayed, side doors to each seating bay
Weight: 29 tons
Seats: 2nd, 106

M59649	M59654	M59659
M59650	M59655	M59660
M59651	M59656	M59661
M59652	M59657	M59662
M59653	M59658	M59663

SR Class 202 Hastings 6-car unit No. 1015 [*B. Morrison*

Class 177 (4 Suburban) ■
Derby Works, B.R.
Trailer Composite (L)
Introduced: 1960
Body: 63′ 8¾″ × 9′ 3″. Non-gangwayed, side doors to each seating bay
Weight: 30 tons
Seats: 1st, 30; **2nd**, 40

M59664	M59669	M59674
M59665	M59670	M59675
M59666	M59671	M59676
M59667	M59672	M59677
M59668	M59673	M59678

Class 179 (3 Cross Country) ■
Swindon Works, B.R.
Trailer Buffet Second (L)
Introduced: 1959
For details see M59255

SC59679*	SC59682*	SC59684*
SC59680*	SC59683*R	SC59685*
SC59681*		

Class 171 (3) ■
Metropolitan-Cammell
Trailer Composite (L)
Introduced: 1959
For details see M59114

SC59686	SC59689R	SC59691
SC59687R	SC59690R	SC59692R
SC59688		

Class 163 (3) ■
Birmingham R. C. & W. Co.
Trailer Second (L)
Introduced: 1961
Body: 57′ 6″ × 9′ 3″
Weight: 24 tons (24 tons 10 cwt*)
Seats: 2nd, 72

E59693	E59699	E59707
E59694	E59700	E59708
E59695	E59701	E59709
E59696	E59702	E59710
E59697	E59703	E59711
E59698	E59704	E59712

Class 173 (4 Suburban) ■
Derby Works, B.R.
Trailer Second
Introduced: 1960
For details see M59649

M59713	M59715	M59717
M59714	M59716	M59718

Class 177 (4 Suburban) ■
Derby Works, B.R.
Trailer Composite (L)
Introduced: 1960
For details see M59664

M59719	M59721	M59723
M59720	M59722	M59724

Class 173 (4 Suburban) ■
Derby Works, B.R.
Trailer Second
Introduced: 1960
For details see M59649

M59725	M59732	M59738
M59726	M59733	M59739
M59727	M59734	M59740
M59728	M59735	M59741
M59729	M59736	M59743
M59730	M59737	M59744
M59731		

Class 177 (4 Suburban) ■
Derby Works, B.R.
Trailer Composite (L)
Introduced: 1960
For details see M59664

SR Class 205 Hampshire 3-car unit No. 1124 at Netley [J. Scrace

M59745	M59752	M59759
M59746	M59753	M59760
M59747	M59754	M59761
M59748	M59755	M59762
M59749	M59756	M59763
M59750	M59757	M59764
M59751	M59758	

Class 180 (5 Trans-Pennine) ■
Swindon Works, B.R.
Trailer Second (L)
Introduced: 1960
Body: 64′ 6″ × 9′ 3″
Weight: 32 tons
Seats: 2nd, 64

E59765	E59768	E59771
E59766	E59769	E59772
E59767	E59770	E59773

Class 161 (3) ■
Derby Works, B.R.
Trailer Second (L)
Introduced: 1960
For details see E59380

SC59782	SC59791	SC59800
SC59783	SC59792	SC59801
SC59784	SC59793	SC59802
SC59785	SC59794	SC59803
SC59786	SC59795	SC59804
SC59787	SC59796	SC59805
SC59788	SC59797	SC59806
SC59789	SC59798	SC59807
SC59790	SC59799	

Class 163 (3) ■
Birmingham R. C. & W. Co.
Trailer Second (L)
Introduced: 1961
For details see E59693

E59808*	E59812*	E59815*
E59809*	E59813*	E59816*
E59810*	E59814*	E59817*
E59811*		

Class 183 (3 or 4 Inter-City) ■
Swindon Works, B.R.
Trailer Composite (K)
Introduced: 1963
Body: 64′ 6″ × 9′ 3″
Weight: 32 tons 3 cwt
Seats: 1st, 24; **2nd**, 24

W59818	W59822	W59825
W59819	E59823	W59826
E59820	W59824	W59827
E59821		

Class 126/2 (3 or 6 Inter-City) ●
Swindon Works, B.R.
Motor Brake Second (L)
Introduced: 1956
For details see SC51030

SC79088*

Class 126/1 (6 Inter-City) ●
Swindon Works, B.R.
Motor Second (L)
Introduced: 1957
For details see SC50936

SC79168

Class 188 (3 or 6 Inter-City) ●
Swindon Works, B.R.
Trailer First (K)
Introduced: 1957
Body: 64′ 6″ × 9′ 3″. Side corridor with seven first class compartments and end doors
Weight: 33 tons 8 cwt
Seats: 1st, 42

SC79470 SC79479

S.R. DIESEL-ELECTRIC MULTIPLE-UNITS

Class 201 (6S) (6)
Hastings Six-Car Units

Gangwayed within set
Built Eastleigh Works BR from 1957

Motor Saloon Brake Second

Engine:
English Electric 4-cycl type 4SRKT Mark II of 500 b.h.p. at 850 r.p.m.
Body: 58′ 0″ × 8′ 2½″ & 9′ 0″
Weight: 54 tons 2 cwt
Seats: 2nd, 22
Transmission:
Electric. Two nose-suspended axle-hung traction motors
Nos. S60000/1/8–13

Trailer Saloon Second (L)

Body: 58′ 0″ × 8′ 2½″ & 9′ 0″
Weight: 29 tons
Seats: 2nd, 52
Nos. S60500–2/11–19

Trailer First (K)

Body: 58′ 0″ × 8′ 2½″ & 9′ 0″
Weight: 30 tons
Seats: 1st, 42
Nos. S60700/3–5

Trailer Saloon Second (L)

Body: 58′ 0″ × 8′ 2½″ & 9′ 0″
Weight: 29 tons
Seats: 2nd, 52

Trailer Saloon Second (L)

Body: 58′ 0″ × 8′ 2½″ & 9′ 0″
Weight: 29 tons
Seats: 2nd, 52

Motor Saloon Brake Second
(As Above)

1001 1006 1007
1005

Class 202 (6L) (6)
Hastings Six-Car Units

Gangwayed within set
Built Eastleigh Works BR from 1957

Motor Saloon Brake Second

Engine:
English Electric 4-cyl type 4SRKT Mark II of 500 b.h.p. at 850 r.p.m.
Body: 64′ 6″ × 8′ 2½″ & 9′ 0″
Weight: 55 tons
Seats: 2nd, 30
Transmission:
Electric. Two nose-suspended axle-hung traction motors
Nos. S60014–35

Trailer Saloon Second (L)
(*Trailer Second (K))

Body: 64′ 6″ (58′ 0″*) × 8′ 2½″ & 9′ 0″
Weight: 30 tons
Seats: 2nd, 60 (56*)
Nos. S60521–49/51/2
(S60701/2*)

Trailer Saloon Second (L)
(*Trailer Second (K))

Body: 64′ 6″ (58′ 0″*) × 8′ 2½″ & 9′ 0″
Weight: 30 tons
Seats: 2nd, 60 (56*)

Trailer First (K)

Body: 64′ 6″ × 8′ 2½″ & 9′ 0″
Weight: 31 tons
Seats: 1st, 48
Nos. S60707–17

Trailer Saloon Second (L)

Body: 64′ 6″ × 8′ 2½″ & 9′ 0″
Weight: 30 tons
Seats: 2nd, 60

SR Class 206 Reading–Redhill unit No. 1206 [*J. Scrace*

SR Class 207 East Sussex unit No. 1314 [*L. Bertram*

Motor Saloon Brake Second
(As Above)

1011	1015	1019
1012	1016	1031
1013	1017	1032*
1014	1018	

Motor Saloon Brake Second
(As Above)

1033	1035	1037
1034	1036	

Class 203 (6B) (6) Hastings Six-Car Units

Gangwayed within set
Built 1958, Eastleigh Works BR

Motor Saloon Brake Second
Engine:
English Electric 4-cyl type 4SRKT Mark II of 500 b.h.p. at 850 r.p.m.
Body: 64′ 6″ × 8′ 2½″ & 9′ 0″
Weight: 55 tons
Seats: 2nd, 30
Transmission:
Electric. Two nose-suspended axle-hung traction motors
Nos. S60036–45

Trailer Saloon Second (L)
Body: 64′ 6″ × 8′ 2½″ & 9′ 0″
Weight: 30 tons
Seats: 2nd, 60
Nos. S60550/3–61

Trailer Buffet
Body: 64′ 6″ × 8′ 2½″ & 9′ 0″
Weight: 35 tons
Seats: Buffett, 21
Nos. S60751–4/6

Trailer First (K)
Body: 64′ 6″ × 8′ 2½″ & 9′ 0″
Weight: 31 tons
Seats: 1st, 48
Nos. S60718–22

Trailer Saloon Second (L)
(As Above)

Class 205 Hampshire† and Berkshire‡ 3-car units Class 204 Hastings 2-car units*

Built 1957 Eastleigh Works BR

Motor Open Brake Second
Engine:
English Electric 4-cyl type 4SRKT Mark II of 600 b.h.p. at 850 r.p.m.
Body: 64 0″ × 9′ 3″
Weight: 56 tons
Seats: 2nd, 52 (42‡)
Transmission:
Electric. Two nose-suspended axle-hung traction motors
Nos. S60100–25/45–51

Trailer Semi-open Second
In 3-car units only
Body: 63′ 6″ × 9′ 3″
Weight: 30 tons
Seats: 2nd, 104
Nos. S60650–78

Driving Trailer Composite (L)
Body: 64′ 0″ × 9′ 3″. Non-gangwayed, side doors to each seating bay or compartment. 5-bay 2nd class saloon and 2 1st class compartments with intermediate lavatories, also a 2nd class compartment next to driving compartment. A luggage compartment has been fitted in place of the 2nd class compartment in the Hampshire units

Weight: 32 tons
Seats: **1st**, 13; **2nd**, 50 (62*‡)
Nos. S60800–32

1101†	1112†	1123†
1102†	1113†	1124†
1103†	1114†	1125†
1104†	1115†	1126†
1105†	1116†	1127‡
1106†	1117†	1128‡
1107†	1118†	1129‡
1108†	1119*	1130‡
1109†	1120*	1131‡
1110†	1121*	1132‡
1111†	1122*	1133‡

Class 206 (3R) (3)
Reading-Redhill Three-Car Units

Formed 1964 from ex-Hastings motor and trailer cars and ex-EMU driving trailers

Motor Saloon Brake Second

Engine:
English Electric 4-cyl type 4SRKT Mark II of 500 b.h.p. at 850 r.p.m.
Body: 58′ 0″×8′ 2½″ & 9′ 0″
Weight: 54 tons 2 cwt
Seats: **2nd**, 22
Transmission:
Electric. Two nose-suspended axle-hung traction motors
Nos. S60002–7

Trailer Saloon Second (L)

Body: 58′ 0″×8′ 2½″ & 9′ 0″
Weight: 29 tons
Seats: **2nd**, 52
Nos. S60503–6/9/10

Driving Trailer Semi-Compartment Second

Body: 63′ 11½″×9′ 0″ & 9′ 3″
Weight: 30 tons
Seats: **2nd**, 66
Nos. S77500/3/7–10

1201	1203	1205
1202	1204	1206

Class 207 (3D) (3)
East Sussex Three-Car Units

Built 1962 Eastleigh Works BR

Motor Open Brake Second

Engine:
English Electric 4-cyl type 4SRKT Mark II of 600 b.h.p. at 850 r.p.m.
Body: 64′ 0″×8′ 6″ & 9′ 0″
Weight: 56 tons
Seats: **2nd**, 42
Transmission:
Electric. Two nose-suspended axle-hung traction motors
Nos. S60126–44

Trailer Composite (L)

Body: 63′ 6″×8′ 6″ & 9′ 0″. Non-gangwayed, side doors to each seating bay or compartment. 3-bay 2nd class saloon, 4 1st class compartments, side lavatory and further 2-bay 2nd class saloon connected by side corridors.
Weight: 31 tons
Seats: **1st**, 24; **2nd**,42
Nos. S60600–18

Driving Trailer Semi-Open Second

Body: 64′ 0″×8′ 6″ & 9′ 0″
Weight: 32 tons
Seats: **2nd**, 76
Nos. S60900–18

1301	1308	1314
1302	1309	1315
1303	1310	1316
1304	1311	1317
1305	1312	1318
1306	1313	1319
1307		

BRITISH RAILWAYS HIGH-SPEED TRAIN

Following trials of the experimental HST unit 252 001, introduced in 1972 and now withdrawn, HST services have been introduced on the Western Region and are shortly to begin on the Eastern Region. The sets consist of a rake of Mk. III coaches with a lightweight power car at each end. The units can be easily remarshalled as required. The vehicles are therefore shown by their unit numbers in this section. The power cars are listed separately in *Abc BR Diesel Locomotives* (or the Diesel Locomotives section of the Combined Volume).

Classes 253 and 254
7 or 8 cars (+2 power cars) to each train

Class 253: Built 1976–7. Production 7-car units for Western Region. 14 further units on order
Class 254: Built 1977 and currently in production. 8-car units for Eastern Region

POWER CARS
Engine: Paxman Valenta 12-cyl. 12RP200L V-type, super-charged and inter-cooled, of 2,250 b.h.p. (1,680 kW)
Weight: 66 tons
Transmission: Four Brush fully suspended traction motors driving through a cardan shaft with flexible couplings and single reduction gearing
Maximum speed: 125 m.p.h.

Class 253

253 001	253 007	253 013
253 002	253 008	253 014
253 003	253 009	253 015
253 004	253 010	253 016
253 005	253 011	253 017
253 006	253 012	253 018
253 019	253 022	253 025
253 020	253 023	253 026
253 021	253 024	253 027

Units ordered for WR West of England services

253 028	253 033	253 038
253 029	253 034	253 039
253 030	253 035	253 040
253 031	253 036	253 041
253 032	253 037	

Class 254

254 001	254 012	254 023
254 002	254 013	254 024
254 003	254 014	254 025
254 004	254 015	254 026
254 005	254 016	254 027
254 006	254 017	254 028
254 007	254 018	254 029
254 008	254 019	254 030
254 009	254 020	254 031
254 010	254 021	254 032
254 011	254 022	

Class 253 High Speed Train power car No. W43011 [*D. Williams*

Restaurant car of a Class 253 High Speed Train [*R. E. Ruffell*

Class 253 High Speed Train No. 253 004 [*S. R. Joyce*

Class 254 High Speed Train No. 254 001 at York [B. Morrison

DEPARTMENTAL DIESEL MULTIPLE-UNITS

Former numbers in brackets

Derby/Cowlairs Works, B.R. (2)

Introduced: 1958
Electrical equipment: Two 100kW Siemens-Schuckert nose-suspended traction motors powered by 216 lead-acid cell batteries of 1070 amp/hour capacity
Body: 57′ 6″×9′ 2″

DB975003 (SC79998)
DB975004 (SC79999)

D. Wickham & Co. (2)

Introduced: 1957 as motor brake second and driving trailer composite*. Converted 1967 for use as General Manager's Saloon
Engines:
Two B.U.T. (Leyland) 6-cyl horizontal type of 150 b.h.p.
Body: 57′ 0″×9′ 3″ (57′ 6″×9′ 3″*)
Transmission:
Mechanical. Standard

DB975005 (E50416)
DB975006* (E56171)

Derby Works, B.R. (2)

Ultrasonic Test Train
Introduced: 1954 as motor brake second and driving trailer composite*
Engines:
Two B.U.T. (A.E.C.) 6-cyl horizontal type of 150 b.h.p.
Body: 57′ 0″×9′ 3″ (57′ 6″×9′ 3″*)
Transmission:
Mechanical. Standard

DB975007 (M79018)
DB975008* (M79612)

Derby Works, B.R. ♦

Introduced: 1956 as motor brake second single-unit
Engines:
Two B.U.T. (A.E.C.) 6-cyl horizontal type of 150 b.h.p.
Body: 57′ 6″ × 9′ 2″. Non-gangwayed. Driving compartment at each end
Transmission:
Mechanical. Standard

RDB975010 (M79900)

Derby Works, B.R. ♦

Introduced: 1955 as driving trailer composite
Body: 57′ 6″×9′ 2″
DB975013 (E79250)

Metropolitan-Cammell (2)♦

Introduced: 1955 as motor brake second
Engines:
Two B.U.T. (A.E.C.) 6-cyl horizontal type of 150 b.h.p.
Body: 57′ 0″×9′ 3″
Transmission:
Mechanical. Standard

DB975018 (E79047)
DB975019 (E79053)

Gloucester R.C. & W. Co. ■

Introduced: 1958 as motor brake second single-unit
Engines:
Two B.U.T. (A.E.C.) 6-cyl horizontal type of 150 b.h.p.

Body: 64′ 6″ × 9′ 3″. Non-gangwayed, side doors to each seating bay
Transmission:
Mechanical. Standard

TDB975023 (W55001)
DB975042 (M55019)
DB975227 (M55017)
TDB975309
TDB975310
TDB975540 (W55016)

Park Royal Vehicles (2) ■

Introduced: 1957 as motor brake second and driving trailer composite*
Engines:
Two B.U.T. (A.E.C.) 6-cyl horizontal type of 150 b.h.p.
Body: 57′ 6″ × 9′ 3″
Transmission:
Mechanical. Standard

DB975089 (M50396)
DB975137* (M50397)
DB975090 (M56162)
DB975228* (M56160)

Swindon Works, B.R. ■

Introduced: 1963 as trailer buffet second
Body: 64′ 6″ × 9′ 3″
TDB975327 (W59828)

Gloucester R.C. & W. Co. ■

Introduced: 1957 as motor brake second
Engines:
Two B.U.T. (A.E.C.) 6-cyl horizontal type of 150 b.h.p.
Body: 57′ 6″ × 9′ 3″
Transmission:
Mechanical. Standard

DB975349 (E51116)

Class 129 ♦
Cravens

Introduced: 1958 as motor parcels van
Engines:
Two B.U.T. (A.E.C.) 6-cyl horizontal type of 150 b.h.p.
Body: 57′ 6″ × 9′ 3″
Non-gangwayed
Transmission:
Mechanical. Standard

RDB975385 (M55997)

Class 203
Eastleigh Works, B.R.

Introduced: 1958 as trailer buffet
Body: 64′ 6″ × 8′ 2½ & 9′ 0″

RDB975386 (S60750)

Swindon Works, B.R. ●

Introduced: 1956 as motor brake second
Engines:
Two B.U.T. (A.E.C.) 6-cyl horizontal type of 150 b.h.p.
Body: 64′ 6″ × 9′ 3″
Transmission:
Mechanical. Standard

ADM975426 (SC79098)

Derby Works, B.R. ■

Introduced: 1955 as driving trailer composite. Subsequently modified internally for use as an inspection saloon including a pantry
Body: 57′ 6″ × 9′ 2″

DB999510 (M79649)

LATE INFORMATION

Correct to 31 December.

Withdrawn: 51126, 56248.

Reclassified: 59486 now Class 190.

Fitted with Leyland engines: 51058/72/85/7.

ELECTRIC LOCOMOTIVES AND MULTIPLE UNITS

Although no new electric locomotives have been built during 1977 there have been a number of developments in electric motive power. Inflexibility has proved to be the downfall of SR Class 71 locomotives, and many of these and the Class 74 electro-diesels are now out of service. These may be stored or withdrawn in due course, but so far only 74 002/6 have been scrapped. The LMR has withdrawn some members of class 76, although others have been fitted with train air brakes and jumper cables for mu working. One member of the class, No. 76 020, is to be preserved at the National Railway Museum, York. The Queen's Silver Jubilee brought a surprise announcement from BR that all the Class 87 locomotives are to be named. So far, 87001 has been named Royal Scot, while 87 101 has received the Stephenson plates originally carried by 87 001 and Nos. 87 005–9 have also been officially named.

Multiple units of Class 312 continue to be delivered to the Eastern Region for GN outer suburban services, those for the GN lines having received the blue and grey "main line" livery. Further SR units have been converted into the 2-SAP Class and new 4-EPBs have been formed from 2-SAP motor cars and spare trailers. Some withdrawn 4-SUB motor coaches have been reappearing paired as departmental de-icing units.

The first prototype Advanced Passenger Train power car (APT-P) is undergoing trials on the WCML and although formations are uncertain at present, the coach number series and proposed unit numbers are shown under Class 370.

Electric locomotives on BR were originally numbered in two series. Those built to BR designs were numbered from E3000 for a.c. units and from E5000 for d.c. units. Earlier locomotives built to pre-Nationalisation designs were numbered in the 20000 series. To allow for computerisation, an entirely new five figure numbering scheme was introduced in 1972.

In this new system, the locomotive class number is followed by an individual identification number and the book lists locomotives in the new number order.

The headings to each class show the type designation or class the manufacturers of main components, the type of train heating, and the previous number series.

Wheel arrangements of electric (and diesel) locomotives are described by a development of the Continental notation. This calculates by axles and not by wheels, and uses letters instead of numerals to denote driving axles ("A"=1, "B"=2, "C"=3, etc.) and numerals only for non-powered axles.

If all axles on a bogie or frame unit are individually powered, a suffix letter "o" is added to the descriptive letter. Thus BR electric locomotive No. 71 001 is shown as a Bo-Bo, indicating that it has two four-wheel bogies, each axle of which has an individual traction motor.

The type of train braking is shown in the details for each class.

Electric multiple-unit trains are listed Region by Region and sub-divided into areas or lines or, in the case of the SR, into types of stock. Details of all coaches in each type of set are listed together. The dimensions shown are length and width over body and width overall. The standard coach descriptions have been used but some additional terms have been introduced to indicate detail differences. The term "semi-open" indicates a basically open vehicle divided into two smaller units by a solid transverse partition; the term "semi-compartment" indicates a vehicle with some open and some compartment accommodation. The term "saloon" has been reserved for low-density open vehicles with large windows to each seating bay, main line standard four-a-side seating and end doors, while the term "open" indicates a high density open vehicle with suburban five-a-side seating and doors to each seating bay or a high-density open vehicle with air-operated sliding doors. The letter (L) in the headings indicates an open vehicle fitted with toilet facilities, (K) indicates a side corridor vehicle with toilet and (H) indicates a vehicle with open or saloon second class accommodation, side corridor first class accommodation and a toilet. All motor coaches have driving facilities unless the heading specifically states otherwise.

Unit numbers, which are painted on the front and rear of each set, are listed where used by BR, together with the number series of individual coaches (these may have gaps due to scrapping, etc.). Where unit numbers are not used by BR, coach numbers only are shown.

The numbers of electric locomotives and multiple units in service have been checked to the following dates: LMR 27 November, ER 27 November, SR 17 October, WR 26 November, SCR 26 November.

Alterations are shown each month in *Modern Railways* and *Railway World*.

Information in this booklet has been checked against BR TOPS records.

ELECTRIC LOCOMOTIVES

Class 71 Bo-Bo

Introduced 1958 for Southern Region. Third rail 750 V. d.c. collection and fitted pantograph for 750 V. d.c. overhead in yards. All stored.
Equipment: Motor generator booster set and four English Electric 532 traction motors
Maximum rail h.p.: 3,000 h.p.
Mechanical parts: BR
Weight: 77 tons
Brake force: 41 tons. Dual braked
Maximum tractive effort: 43,000 lb
Route availability: 6
Maximum speed: 90 m.p.h.
Electric train heating (Night Ferry stock only)
Previous no. series: E5000–5023
See also Class 74

71 001	71 006	71 011
71 002	71 007	71 012
71 003	71 008	71 013
71 004	71 009	71 014
71 005	71 010	

TOTAL: 14

Class 73 Bo-Bo

Electro-diesel locos built 1962* (1965) to operate from SR 750 V. d.c. third rail or on diesel engine
Equipment: English Electric 4-cyl. type 4 SRKT Mk. 2 600 b.h.p. diesel engine; four English Electric 542A traction motors
Total h.p.: Electric 2,450, Diesel 600
Mechanical parts: BR, English Electric
Weight: *75 tons, 76 tons
Brake force: 31 tons. Dual braked and EP braking
Maximum tractive effort: 42,000 lb
Route availability: 6
Maximum speed: *80, 90 m.p.h.

***Class 73/0**

73 001	73 003	73 005
73 002	73 004	73 006

TOTAL: 6

Class 73/1

73 101	73 115	73 129
73 102	73 116	73 130
73 103	73 117	73 131
73 104	73 118	73 132
73 105	73 119	73 133
73 106	73 120	73 134
73 107	73 121	73 135
73 108	73 122	73 136
73 109	73 123	73 137
73 110	73 124	73 138
73 111	73 125	73 139
73 112	73 126	73 140
73 113	73 127	73 141
73 114	73 128	73 142

TOTAL: 42

Class 74 Bo-Bo

Electro-diesels rebuilt in 1968 from Class 71 locomotives to operate from SR 750 V. d.c. third rail or on diesel engine. Most now in store or withdrawn
Equipment: Paxman 6-cyl. type 6YJXL 650 b.h.p. diesel engine; four English Electric 532A spring-borne traction motors
Total h.p.: Electric 4,600, Diesel 650
Mechanical parts: BR
Weight: 85 tons
Brake force: 69 tons. Dual braked

Class 71 Bo-Bo No. 71 007 [*B. Morrison*

Class 73 Electro-Diesel Bo-Bo No. 73 005 [*J. Scrace*

Maximum tractive effort: 40,000 lb
Route availability: 7
Maximum speed: 90 m.p.h.
Electric train heating
Previous no. series: E6101–6110

74 001	74 005	74 009
74 003	74 007	74 010
74 004	74 008	

TOTAL: 8

Class 76 Bo-Bo

Built 1950 for Manchester–Sheffield 1,500 V. d.c. overhead electrification. Locomotives fitted with train air brakes (¶ or ●) are also equipped for multiple-unit operation with other Class 76 locomotives
Equipment: Four Metro-Vick 186 traction motors of 1,300 h.p. (970 kW)
Mechanical parts: BR
Maximum rail h.p.: 3,300
Weight: 87/88 tons
Brake force: 73 tons. Vacuum brake (¶ Dual braked. ● Air braked)
Maximum tractive effort: 45,000 lb
Route availability: 8
Maximum speed: 65 m.p.h.
No train heating
Previous no. series: E26001–26057

76 001 76 002
76 003 (76 036)

76 004	76 013¶	76 024¶
76 006¶	76 014¶	76 025¶
76 007¶	76 015¶	76 026¶
76 008¶	76 016¶	76 027¶
76 009¶	76 021¶	76 028¶
76 010¶	76 022¶	76 029¶
76 011¶	76 023¶	76 030¶
76 012¶		

76 031● (76 036)
76 032● 76 033 76 034●
76 035● (76 018)
76 036 (76 003)
76 037●
76 038● (76 050)
76 039 (76 048)

76 040	76 047	76 053
76 041	76 049	76 054
76 043	76 051	76 058
76 046	76 052	

TOTAL: 45

Class 81 Bo-Bo

Introduced 1959 for LMR Western Lines 25 kV overhead electrification
Equipment: A.E.I. (B.T.H.). Four A.E.I. (B.T.H.) 189 spring-borne d.c. traction motors driving through Alsthom quill drive. 3,200 h.p. (2,387 kW) continuous rating
Mechanical parts: BRCW
Weight: 78 tons.
Brake force: 69 tons. Dual braked
Maximum tractive effort: 50, 000 lb
Route availability: 6
Maximum speed: 100 m.p.h.
Electric train heating
Previous no. series: E3001–3023, E3096/3097

81 001	81 009	81 016
81 002	81 010	81 017
81 003	81 011	81 018
81 004	81 012	81 019
81 005	81 013	81 020
81 006	81 014	81 021
81 007	81 015	81 022
81 008		

TOTAL: 22

Class 82 Bo-Bo

Introduced in 1960 for LMR Western Lines 25 kV electrification
Equipment: A.E.I. (M.V.) Four A.E.I. 189 d.c. traction motors driving through Alsthom quill drive. 3,300 h.p. continuous (2,462 kW) rating

Class 74 Electro-Diesel Bo-Bo No. 74 004 [*B. Morrison*

Class 76 Bo-Bo No. 76 023 [*J. C. Hillmer*

Mechanical parts: Metropolitan Vickers
Weight: 78½ tons
Brake force: 67 tons. Dual braked
Maximum tractive effort: 50,000 lb
Route availability: 6
Maximum speed: 100 m.p.h.
Electric train heating
Previous no. series: E3047–3054

82 001	82 004	82 007
82 002	82 005	82 008
82 003	82 006	

TOTAL: 8

Class 83 Bo-Bo

Introduced in 1960 for LMR Western Lines 25 kV electrification
Equipment: E.E. Four English Electric 535A spring-borne d.c. traction motors driving through S.L.M. resilient drives. 2,950 kV (2,200 kW) continuous rating
Mechanical parts: English Electric
Weight: 75 tons
Brake force: 71 tons. Dual braked
Maximum tractive effort: 38,000 lb
Route availability: 6
Maximum speed: 100 m.p.h.
Electric train heating
Previous no. series: E3024–3035, E3098–3100

83 001	83 006	83 011
83 002	83 007	83 012
83 003	83 008	83 013
83 004	83 009	83 014
83 005	83 010	83 015

TOTAL: 15

Class 84 Bo-Bo

Introduced in 1960 for LMR Western Lines 25 kV electrification
Equipment: G.E.C. Four G.E.C. WT 501 spring-borne d.c. traction motors driving through Brown-Boveri spring drives. 3,100 h.p. (2,313 kW) continuous rating
Mechanical parts: North British
Weight: 75½ tons
Brake force: 69 tons. Dual braked
Maximum tractive effort: 50,000 lb
Route availability: 6
Maximum speed: 100 m.p.h.
Electric train heating
Previous no. series: E3036–3045

84 001	84 006	84 009
84 002	84 008	84 010
84 003		

Scheduled for early withdrawal.

TOTAL: 7

Class 85 Bo-Bo

Introduced in 1960 for LMR Western Lines 25 kV electrification
Equipment: A.E.I. Four A.E.I. (B.T.H.) 189 d.c. traction motors driving through Alsthom quill drive. 3,200 h.p. (2387 kW) continuous rating
Mechanical parts: BR
Weight: 81 tons
Brake force: 71 tons. Dual braked
Maximum tractive effort: 50,000 lb
Route availability: 6
Maximum speed: 100 m.p.h.
Electric train heating
Previous no. series: E3056–3095

85 001	85 010	85 019
85 002	85 011	85 020
85 003	85 012	85 021
85 004	85 013	85 022
85 005	85 014	85 023
85 006	85 015	85 024
85 007	85 016	85 025
85 008	85 017	85 026
85 009	85 018	85 027

Class 81 Bo-Bo No. 81 004 [*B. J. Nicolle*

Class 82 Bo-Bo No. 82 008 [*B. J. Nicolle*

85 028	85 033	85 037
85 029	85 034	85 038
85 030	85 035	85 039
85 031	85 036	85 040
85 032		

TOTAL: 40

Class 86 — Bo-Bo

Introduced 1965 for LMR Western Lines 25 kV a.c. system
Equipment: E.E./A.E.I. Four A.E.I. type 282AZ nose-suspended traction motors. 3,600 h.p. (2,686 kW) continuous rating (Class 86/0 only)
Mechanical parts: English Electric and B.R.
Weight: 81½–82½ tons
Brake force: 68 tons. Dual braked
Maximum tractive effort: 58,000 lb
Route availability: 6
Maximum speed: 100 m.p.h.
Electric train heating
Previous no. series: E3100 series

Class 86/0

86 001	86 014	86 027
86 002	86 015	86 028
86 003	86 016	86 029
86 004	86 017	86 030
86 005	86 018	86 031
86 006	86 019	86 032
86 007	86 020	86 033
86 008	86 021	86 034
86 009	86 022	86 035
86 010	86 023	86 036
86 011	86 024	86 037
86 012	86 025	86 038
86 013	86 026	86 039

TOTAL: 39

Class 86/1

Rebuilt 1972 with BP9 bogies and four spring-borne G.E.C. G412AZ traction motors and Flexicoil suspension. 5,000 h.p. (3,730 kW) continuous rating.
Weight: 85½ tons

86 101 (86 201)
86 102 (86 202)
86 103 (86 203)

TOTAL: 3

Class 86/2

Rebuilt 1972 with Flexicoil suspension and four A.E.I. type 282BZ traction motors. 4,040 h.p. (3,014 kW) continuous rating. Some with resilient wheels
Weight: 83½ tons

86 204	86 221	86 237
86 205	86 222	86 238
86 206	86 223	86 239
86 207	86 224	86 240
86 208	86 225	86 241
86 209	86 226	86 242
86 210	86 227	86 243
86 211	86 228	86 244
86 212	86 229	86 245
86 213	86 230	86 246
86 214	86 231	86 247
86 215	86 232	86 248
86 216	86 233	86 249
86 217	86 234	86 250
86 218	86 235	86 251
86 219	86 236	86 252
86 220		

86 253 (86 044)
86 254 (86 047)
86 255 (86 042)
86 256 (86 040)
86 257 (86 043)
86 258 (86 046)
86 259 (86 045)
86 260 (86 048)
86 261 (86 041)

TOTAL: 58

Class 87/0 — Bo-Bo

Built in 1973 for LMR West Coast main line electrification to Glasgow 25 kV a.c.

Class 83 Bo-Bo No. 83 002 [B. J. Nicolle

Class 85 Bo-Bo No. 85 022 [B. J. Nicolle

Equipment: G.E.C. Four G412AZ traction motors with flexible drive. 5,000 h.p. (3,730 kW) continuous rating
Mechanical parts: BREL
Weight: 82 tons
Brake force: 69 tons. Air braked
Maximum tractive effort: 58,000 lb
Route availability: 6
Maximum speed: 100 m.p.h.
Electric train heating

87 001 Royal Scot
87 002 Royal Sovereign
87 003 Patriot
87 004 Britannia
87 005 City of London
87 006 City of Glasgow
87 007 City of Manchester
87 008 City of Liverpool
87 009 City of Birmingham
87 010 King Arthur
87 011 The Black Prince
87 012 Coeur de Lion
87 013 John o'Gaunt
87 014 Knight of the Thistle
87 015 Howard of Effingham
87 016 Sir Francis Drake
87 017 Iron Duke
87 018 Lord Nelson
87 019 Sir Winston Churchill
87 020 North Briton
87 021 Robert the Bruce
87 022 Cock o' the North
87 023 Highland Chieftain
87 024 Lord of the Isles
87 025 Borderer
87 026 Redgauntlet
87 027 Wolf of Badenoch
87 028 Lord President
87 029 Earl Marischal
87 030 Black Douglas
87 031 Hal o' the Wind
87 032 Kenilworth
87 033 Thane of Fife
87 034 William Shakespeare
87 035 Robert Burns

TOTAL: 35

Class 87/1 **Bo-Bo**

Class 87 locomotive built in 1974 with thyristor control equipment
Equipment: G.E.C. Four G412BZ traction motors with flexible drive. 4,850 h.p. (3,628 kW) continuous rating
Mechanical parts: BREL
Weight: 78 tons

87 101 Stephenson

TOTAL: 1

LATE INFORMATION

Correct to 31 December.

Withdrawn: 28313/5, 28340/69, 29549/86, 29891.

Class 86/2 Bo-Bo No. 86 223 [B. J. Nicolle

Class 87/0 Bo-Bo No. 87 022 [N. E. Preedy

ELECTRIC MULTIPLE-UNITS
London Midland Region

SYSTEM:
630 VOLTS D.C. 3rd RAIL

Class 501
London District Three-Car Sets

B.R. Standard design
Introduced: 1957

Motor Open Brake Second

Body: 57′ 5″×9′ 0″ & 9′ 6″
Seats: 2nd, 74
Weight: 47 tons
Equipment: Four 185 h.p. G.E.C traction motors

M61135	M61153	M61174
M61137	M61154	M61176
M61141	M61155	M61177
M61142	M61156	M61178
M61143	M61157	M61179
M61144	M61158	M61180
M61145	M61159	M61181
M61146	M61160	M61182
M61147	M61163	M61183
M61148	M61164	M61184
M61149	M61168	M61185
M61150	M61169	M61186
M61151	M61170	M61188
M61152	M61171	M61189

Trailer Second
(*Trailer Open Second
†Trailer Semi-Open Second)

Body: 57′ 1″×9′ 0″ & 9′ 6″
Seats: 2nd, 108 (92*, 94†)
Weight: 29 tons

M70135*	M70142*	M70145†
M70137†	M70143†	M70146†
M70141*	M70144*	M70148*
M70149†	M70161*	M70178*
M70150*	M70163*	M70179*
M70152†	M70164*	M70180*
M70153*	M70167	M70181*
M70154†	M70168†	M70182†
M70155†	M70169†	M70183*
M70156*	M70170*	M70184†
M70157†	M70171*	M70185†
M70158*	M70174*	M70186*
M70159†	M70176*	M70188*
M70160†	M70177*	M70189†

Driving Trailer Open Brake Second

Body: 57′ 5″×9′ 0″ & 9′ 6″
Seats: 2nd, 74
Weight: 30 tons

M75135	M75154	M75174
M75137	M75155	M75176
M75141	M75156	M75177
M75142	M75157	M75178
M75143	M75158	M75179
M75144	M75159	M75180
M75145	M75160	M75181
M75146	M75161	M75182
M75148	M75163	M75183
M75149	M75164	M75184
M75150	M75168	M75185
M75151	M75169	M75186
M75152	M75170	M75188
M75153	M75171	M75189

Class 501 3-car unit passing Bushey on a Watford–Euston working [*B. Morrison*

Class 502 5-car unit refurbished in Manchester PTE livery [*R. T. Foster*

SYSTEM:
600/750 VOLTS D.C. 3rd RAIL

Class 502
Liverpool-Southport Three- and Five-Car Sets

With air-operated sliding doors
Introduced: 1939

Motor Open Brake Second

Body: 66′ 6″×9′ 3″ & 9′ 5″
Seats: 2nd, 88
Weight: 42 tons
Equipment: Four 235 h.p. English Electric traction motors

M28311M	M28333M	M28353M
M28312M	M28334M	M28354M
M28313M	M28335M	M28355M
M28314M	M28337M	M28356M
M28315M	M28338M	M28357M
M28318M	M28339M	M28358M
M28319M	M28340M	M28359M
M28322M	M28341M	M28360M
M28323M	M28343M	M28361M
M28326M	M28347M	M28362M
M28328M	M28349M	M28364M
M28330M	M28351M	M28366M
M28331M	M28352M	M28369M
M28332M		

Trailer Open Second

Body: 66′ 6″×9′ 3″ & 9′ 5″
Seats: 2nd, 102
Weight: 24 tons

M29545M	M29546M	M29547M
M29548M	M29566M	M29584M
M29549M	M29567M	M29585M
M29552M	M29568M	M29586M
M29554M	M29570M	M29587M
M29555M	M29573M	M29588M
M29556M	M29574M	M29589M
M29557M	M29577M	M29591M
M29559M	M29578M	M29593M
M29560M	M29579M	M29595M
M29561M	M29580M	M29598M
M29562M	M29581M	M29599M
M29564M	M29582M	
M29565M	M29583M	

Driving Trailer Open Second

Body: 66′ 6″×9′ 3″ & 9′ 5″
Seats: 2nd, 78
Weight: 25 tons

M29862M	M29874M	M29886M
M29863M	M29875M	M29887M
M29864M	M29876M	M29888M
M29865M	M29877M	M29889M
M29866M	M29878M	M29890M
M29867M	M29879M	M29891M
M29868M	M29880M	M29892M
M29869M	M29881M	M29893M
M29870M	M29882M	M29894M
M29871M	M29883M	M29895M
M29872M	M29884M	M29896M
M29873M	M29885M	M29897M

SYSTEM
600/750 VOLTS D.C. 3rd RAIL

Class 503
Wirral and Mersey Three-Car Sets

With air-operated sliding doors
Introduced: 1938 and 1956

Motor Open Brake Second

Body: 58′ 0″×8′ 8″ & 9′ 11″
Seats: 2nd, 56
Weight: 36 or 37 tons
Equipment: Four 135 h.p. B.T.H. traction motors

M28371M	M28386M	M28677M
M28372M	M28387M	M28678M
M28373M	M28388M	M28679M
M28374M	M28389M	M28680M
M28375M	M28390M	M28681M
M28376M	M28391M	M28682M
M28377M	M28392M	M28683M
M28378M	M28393M	M28684M
M28379M	M28394M	M28685M
M28380M	M28672M	M28686M
M28381M	M28673M	M28687M
M28382M	M28674M	M28688M
M28383M	M28675M	M28689M
M28384M	M28676M	M28690M
M28385M		

M28371–94M are 1956 cars

Trailer Open Second

Body: 56′ 0″×8′ 8″ & 9′ 11″
Seats: 2nd, 55
Weight: 20 or 21 tons

M29702M	M29703M	M29704M
M29705M	M29821M	M29834M
M29706M	M29822M	M29835M
M29707M	M29823M	M29836M
M29709M	M29824M	M29837M
M29710M	M29825M	M29838M
M29711M	M29826M	M29839M
M29712M	M29827M	M29840M
M29713M	M29828M	M29841M
M29714M	M29829M	M29842M
M29715M	M29830M	M29843M
M29716M	M29831M	M29844M
M29718M	M29832M	M29845M
M29719M	M29833M	M29846M
M29720M		

M29821–46M are 1956 cars

Driving Trailer Open Second

Body: 58′ 0″×8′ 8″ & 9′ 11″
Seats: 2nd, 66
Weight: 21 tons

M29131M	M29146M	M29274M
M29132M	M29147M	M29275M
M29133M	M29148M	M29276M
M29134M	M29149M	M29278M
M29135M	M29150M	M29279M
M29136M	M29151M	M29280M
M29137M	M29152M	M29281M
M29138M	M29153M	M29282M
M29139M	M29154M	M29283M
M29140M	M29155M	M29284M
M29141M	M29156M	M29285M
M29142M	M29271M	M29287M
M29143M	M29272M	M29288M
M29144M	M29273M	M29289M
M29145M		

M29131–56M are 1956 cars

A Manchester–Bury train formed of two Class 504 2-car units

SYSTEM:
1,200 VOLTS D.C. SIDE CONTACT 3rd RAIL

Class 504
Manchester-Bury Two-Car Sets

B.R. Standard design
Introduced: 1959

Motor Open Brake Second

Body: 63′ 11½×9′ 0″ & 9′ 3″
Seats: 2nd, 84
Weight: 49 tons
Equipment: two 141 h.p. English Electric traction motors

M65436	M65442	M65447
M65437	M65443	M65448
M65438	M65444	M65449
M65439	M65445	M65450
M65441	M65446	M65451
M65452	M65456	M65459
M65453	M65457	M65460
M65454	M65458	M65461
M65455		

Driving Trailer Open Second

Body: 63′ 11½×9′ 0″ & 9′ 3″
Seats: 2nd, 94
Weight: 32 tons

M77157	M77167	M77175
M77158	M77168	M77176
M77159	M77169	M77177
M77160	M77170	M77178
M77162	M77171	M77179
M77163	M77172	M77180
M77165	M77173	M77181
M77166	M77174	M77182

SYSTEM:
1,500 VOLTS D.C. OVERHEAD

Class 506
Manchester-Glossop-Hadfield Three-car Sets

With air-operated sliding doors
Introduced: 1954

Motor Open Brake Second

Body: 60′ 4½×9′ 0″ & 9′ 3″
Seats: 2nd, 52
Weight: 50 tons 12 cwt
Equipment: Four 185 h.p. G.E.C. traction motors

M59401	M59404	M59407
M59402	M59405	M59408
M59403	M59406	

Trailer Open Second

Body: 55′ 0½×9′ 0″ & 9′ 3″
Seats: 2nd, 62
Weight: 26 tons 8 cwt

M59501	M59504	M59507
M59502	M59505	M59508
M59503	M59506	

Driving Trailer Open Second

Body: 55′ 4½″×9′ 0″ & 9′ 3″
Seats: 2nd, 60
Weight: 27 tons 9 cwt

M59601	M59604	M59607
M59602	M59605	M59608
M59603	M59606	

SYSTEM: 600/750 VOLTS D.C. 3rd RAIL

Class 507
Garston-Liverpool-Southport Three-Car Units

B.R. Standard design with air-operated sliding doors
Gangwayed throughout
To be introduced

Motor Open Brake Second

Body: 64′ 11½″ × 9′ 3″
Seats: 2nd, 74
Weight:
Equipment: Eight 110 h.p. GEC traction motors

Trailer Open Second

Body: 65′ 4¼″ × 9′ 3″
Seats: 2nd, 84
Weight:

Motor Open Brake Second
(As above)

507 001	507 014	507 027
507 002	507 015	507 028
507 003	507 016	507 029
507 004	507 017	507 030
507 005	507 018	507 031
507 006	507 019	507 032
507 007	507 020	507 033
507 008	507 021	507 034
507 009	507 022	507 035
507 010	507 023	507 036
507 011	507 024	507 037
507 012	507 025	507 038
507 013	507 026	

SYSTEM: 25 kV A.C. OVERHEAD

Classes 304/1, 304/2* and 304/3†
Euston, Birmingham, Manchester and Liverpool Four-Car Units

B.R. Standard design
Introduced: 1960

Driving Trailer Open Brake Second

Body: 64′ 0⅝″ × 9′ 0″ & 9′ 3″
Seats: 2nd, 82
Weight: 31 tons 8 cwt
(32 tons*†)
Nos.: M75645–79, M75858–67

Trailer Composite (L)

Body: 63′ 6⅛″ × 9′ 0″ & 9′ 3″
Seats: 1st, 19; **2nd,** 60
Weight: 31 tons 5 cwt
Nos.: M70045–59, M70483–502, M70243–52

Non-Driving Motor Brake Second (Open*†)

Body: 63′ 6⅛″ × 9′ 0″ & 9′ 3″
Seats: 2nd, 96 (72*†)
Weight: 53 tons 12 cwt
(54 tons 3 cwt*†)
Equipment: Four A.E.I. 207 h.p. d.c. traction motors
Nos.: M60145–59, M61628–47, M61873–82

Driving Trailer Open Second (L)

Body: 64′ 0⅝″ × 9′ 0″ & 9′ 3″
Seats: 2nd, 80
Weight: 35 tons 12 cwt
Nos.: M75045–59, M75680–99, M75868–77

001	006	011
002	007	012
003	008	013
004	009	014
005	010	015

Class 506 3-car unit with driving trailer open second No. M59607 leading [*B. Morrison*

Class 312/2 4-car unit No. 312 202 at Perry Barr [*W. A. Camwell*

GOLDEN 1928 RCTS **JUBILEE 1978**

The RAILWAY CORRESPONDENCE AND TRAVEL SOCIETY was founded 50 years ago in Cheltenham by a small body of enthusiasts; today the Society is one of the premier organisations of its kind in the country. Membership is available to those over 16 years of age at a cost of £3 for a twelve month period.
The monthly magazine, the *Railway Observer*, is provided for members only: this contains details of the current railway scene, all motive power and rolling stock alterations, preservation, overseas, modern and historical articles. Members are offered meetings, visits, discounts on Society rail tours and discounts on most new Society publications. Two of the most recent publications are:

COACHING STOCK OF BRITISH RAILWAYS (Price £1)
This book gives detailed information and tabulated lists of all BR locomotive-hauled stock, EMU, DMU stock, together with illustrations.

LOCOMOTIVE STOCKBOOK 1977 (Price 80p)
This book gives details of all BR locomotives, detailed alterations, motive power depot allocations, etc.

Remember, the *R.O.* will help to keep your *ABC* and the above publications up-to-date.

The Society also produce a wide range of publications including locomotive histories of the GWR, LNER and SR.

For details of membership and specimen *R.O.*, send 15p in stamps to Dept K, 160 Hillend Crescent, Clarkston, Renfrewshire G76 7XY.

For the above books (sent post free) and full publications list, send to Hon. Asst Publications Officer, Dept K, Rannoch, 72 Upper Way, Upper Longdon, Rugeley, Staffs.

016*	027*	037†
017*	028*	038†
018*	029*	039†
019*	030*	040†
020*	031*	041†
021*	032*	042†
022*	033*	043†
023*	034*	044†
024*	035*	045†
025*	036†	

Class 310
Euston, Birmingham, Manchester and Liverpool Four-Car Units

B.R. Standard design
Partially gangwayed within unit
Introduced: 1966

Driving Trailer Open Second (L)

Body: 65′ $1\frac{5}{8}$″ × 9′ 0″ & 9′ 3″
Seats: 2nd, 80 (*68)
Weight: 36 tons 15 cwt
Nos.: M76130–79

Non-Driving Motor Open Brake Second

Body: 65′ $4\frac{1}{4}$″ × 9′ 0″ & 9′ 3″
Seats: 2nd, 70
Weight: 56 tons 7 cwt
Equipment: Four English Electric 270 h.p. d.c. traction motors
Nos.: M62071–120

Trailer Open Second

Body: 65′ $4\frac{1}{4}$″ × 9′ 0″ & 9′ 3″
Seats: 2nd, 100
Weight: 31 tons 4 cwt
Nos.: M70731–80

Driving Trailer Open Composite (L)

Body: 65′ $1\frac{5}{8}$″ × 9′ 0″ & 9′ 3″
Seats: 1st, 25; **2nd,** 43
Weight: 33 tons 16 cwt
Nos: M76180–229

046	063	080
047	064	081
048	065	082
049	066*	083
050	067	084
051	068	085
052	069	086
053	070	087
054	072	088
055	073	089
056	074	090
057	075	091
058	076	092
059	077	093
060	078	094
061	079	095
062		

Class 370
Advanced Passenger Train Prototype (APT-P)

Six vehicle types are on order to provide up to a possible maximum of six articulated APT units for the WCML 25 kV a.c. electrification. Formations and technical data are not available at present, and both 12- and 14-car formations are likely to be used
Driving Trailer Seconds: Nos. 48101–7
Trailer Seconds: Nos. 48201–12
Trailer Buffet/Restaurant: Nos. 48401–6
Trailer Firsts: Nos. 48501–6
Trailer Brake Firsts: Nos. 48601–7
Motor Coaches (non-driving): Nos. 49001–6

Unit Numbers

370 001	370 003	370 005
370 002	370 004	370 006

Class 311 3-car unit No. 092 leaving Glasgow [B. J. Nicolle

Scottish Region

SYSTEM:
25 and 6.25 kV. A.C. OVERHEAD

Classes 303 and 311† Glasgow Area Three-Car Units

B.R. Standard design with air-operated sliding doors
Introduced: 1960 (1967†)

Driving Trailer Open Second

Body: 63′ 11⅝″ × 9′ 3″ & 9′ 3″
Seats: 2nd, 83
Weight: 34 tons
Nos.: SC75566–600, SC75746–801, SC76403–21

Non-Driving Motor Open Brake Second

Body: 63′ 6⅛″ × 9′ 3″ & 9′ 3″
Seats: 2nd, 70
Weight: 56 tons
Equipment: Four A.E.I. (MV) 207 h.p. d.c. traction motors
†Four AEI 222 h.p. d.c. traction motors
Nos.: SC61481–515, SC61812–67, SC62163–81

Driving Trailer Open Second

Body: 63′ 11⅝″ × 9′ 3″ & 9′ 3″
Seats: 2nd, 83
Weight: 38 tons
Nos.: SC75601–35, SC75802–57, SC76422–40

001	009	017
002	010	018
003	011	019
004	012	020
005	013	021
006	014	022
007	015	023
008	016	024

025	054	083
026	055	084
027	056	085
028	057	086
029	058	087
030	059	088
031	060	089
032	061	090
033	062	091
034	063	092†
035*	064	093†
036	065	094†
037	066	095†
038	067	096†
039	068	097†
040	069	098†
041	070	099†
042	071	100†
043	072	101†
044	073	102†
045	074	103†
046	075	104†
047	076	105†
048	077	106†
049	078	107†
050	079	108†
051	080	109†
052	081	110†
053	082	

*Fitted with thyristor control equipment

Class 314
Glasgow Area Three-Car Units

BR Standard design with air-operated sliding doors gangwayed throughout

To be introduced

Motor Open Brake Second

Body: 64′ 11½″ × 9′ 3″
Seats: 2nd, 74
Weight:
Equipment:

Non-Driving Motor Open Second

Body: 65′ 4¼″ × 9′ 3″
Seats: 2nd, 84
Weight:
Equipment:

Driving Trailer Open Brake Second

Body: 64′ 11½″ × 9′ 3″
Seats: 2nd, 74
Weight:
Equipment:

314 001	314 007	314 012
314 002	314 008	314 013
314 003	314 009	314 014
314 004	314 010	314 015
314 005	314 011	314 016
314 006		

Trailer open brake second of Class 306 3-car unit No. 072 [*P. W. Roynon*

Class 307 4-car unit No. 117 [*B. Morrison*

Eastern Region

SYSTEM:
25kV (and 6.25kV on GE and LT&S) A.C. OVERHEAD

Class 306
Liverpool St.-Shenfield Three-Car Units

With air-operated sliding doors
Introduced: (for d.c. working) 1949;
Rebuilt: (for a.c. working) 1960

Motor Open Second

Body: 60′ 4½″ × 9′ 0″ & 9′ 6″
Seats: 2nd, 62
Weight: 50 tons 17 cwt
Equipment: Four 157 h.p. d.c. traction motors
Nos.: E65201–92

Trailer Open Brake Second

(with transformer and rectifier)
Body: 55′ 0½″ × 9′ 0″ & 9′ 6″
Seats: 2nd, 46
Weight: 26 tons
Nos.: E65401–92

Driving Trailer Open Second

Body: 55′ 4″ × 9′ 0″ & 9′ 6″
Seats: 2nd, 60
Weight: 27 tons 10 cwt
Nos.: E65601–92

001	011	021
002	012	022
003	013	023
004	014	024
005	015	025
006	016	026
007	017	027
008	018	028
009	019	029
010	020	031

032	053	073
033	054	074
034	055	075
035	056	076
036	057	077
037	058	078
038	059	079
039	060	080
040	061	081
041	062	082
042	063	083
043	064	084
044	065	085
045	066	086
046	067	087
047	068	088
048	069	089
049	070	090
050	071	091
051	072	092
052		

Class 307
G.E. Outer Suburban Four-Car Units

B.R. Standard design
Introduced: (for d.c. working) 1956;
Rebuilt: (for a.c. working) 1960.

Driving Trailer Brake Second

(with transformer and rectifier)
Body: 63′ 11½″ × 9′ 0″ & 9′ 3″
Seats: 2nd, 84
Weight:
Nos.: E75001–32

Class 302 4-car unit No. 289 [B. J. Nicolle

Class 305/1 3-car unit No. 439 passing Shenfield [D. Williams

Non-Driving Motor Second

Body: 63′ 6″×9′ 0″ & 9′ 3″
Seats: **2nd**, 120
Weight:
Equipment: Four G.E.C. 174 h.p. d.c. traction motors
Nos.: E61001–32

Trailer Composite (H)

Body: 63′ 6″×9′ 0″ & 9′ 3″
Seats: **1st**, 19; **2nd**, 6
Weight: 30 tons
Nos.: E70001–32

Driving Trailer Open Second (L)

Body: 63′ $11\frac{1}{2}$″×9′ 0″ & 9′ 3″
Seats: **2nd**, 80
Weight:
Nos.: E75101–32

101	112	123
102	113	124
103	114	125
104	115	126
105	116	127
106	117	128
107	118	129
108	119	130
109	120	131
110	121	132
111	122	

Trailer Composite (H)

Body: 63′ 6″×9′ 0″ & 9′ 3″
Seats: **1st**, 19; **2nd**, 60
Weight: 31 tons
Nos.: E70611–43

Non-Driving Motor Brake Second

Body: 63′ 6″×9′ 0″ & 9′ 3″
Seats: **2nd**, 96
Weight: 54 tons
Equipment: Four English Electric 200 h.p. d.c. traction motors
Nos.: E61883–915

Driving Trailer Open Second (L)

Body: 64′ $0\frac{1}{2}$″×9′ 0″ & 9′ 3″
Seats: **2nd**, 80
Weight: 36 tons
Nos.: E75878–86, E75896–919

133	144	155
134	145	156
135	146	157
136	147	158
137	148	159
138	149	160
139	150	161
140	151	162
141	152	163
142	153	164
143	154	165

Class 308/1 G.E. Outer Suburban Four-Car Units

B.R. Standard design
Introduced: 1961

Driving Trailer Second

Body: 64′ $0\frac{1}{2}$″×9′ 0″ & 9′ 3″
Seats: **2nd**, 108
Weight: 32 tons
Nos.: E75887–93, E75929–52

Class 302 Fenchurch St.-Shoeburyness Four-Car Units

B.R. Standard design
Introduced: 1959

Driving Trailer Second

Body: 63′ $11\frac{1}{2}$″×9′ 0″ & 9′ 3″
Seats: **2nd**, 108
Weight: 32 tons
Nos.: E75033–84, E75211–77

Trailer Composite (H)

Body: 63′ 6″ × 9′ 0″ & 9′ 3″
Seats: 1st, 19; **2nd,** 60
Weight: 31 tons
Nos.: E70060–220

Non-Driving Motor Brake Second

Body: 63′ 6″ & 9′ 0″ & 9′ 3″
Seats: 2nd, 96
Weight: 56 tons 10 cwt
Equipment: Four English Electric 192 h.p. d.c. traction motors
Nos.: E61060–132, E61190–220

Driving Trailer Open Second (L)

Body: 63′ 11½″ × 9′ 0″ & 9′ 3″
Seats: 2nd, 80
Weight: 36 tons
Nos.: E75085–100, E75190–352

201	226	251
202	227	252
203	228	253
204	229	254
205	230	255
206	231	256
207	232	257
208	233	258
209	234	259
210	235	260
211	236	261
212	237	262
213	238	263
214	239	264
215	240	265
216	241	266
217	242	267
218	243	268
219	244*	269
220	245	270
221	246	271
222	247	272
223	248	273
224	249	274
225	250	275

276	289	301
277	290	302
278	291	303
279	292	304
280	293	305
281	294	306
282	295	307
283	296	308
284	297	309
285	298	310
286	299	311
287	300	312
288		

*Unit 244 has one ex-Manchester-Bury Class 504 Driving Trailer Open Second

Class 308/4 Fenchurch St.-Shoeburyness Four-Car Units

B.R. Standard design
Introduced: 1961 (Motor coach rebuilt 1971)

Driving Trailer Second

Body: 63′ 11½″ × 9′ 0″ & 9′ 3″
Seats: 2nd, 108
Weight: 32 tons
Nos.: E75953–6

Trailer Composite (H)

Body: 63′ 6″ × 9′ 0″ & 9′ 3″
Seats: 1st, 19; **2nd,** 60
Weight: 31 tons
Nos.: E70644–7

Non-Driving Motor Open Brake Second

Body: 63′ 6″ × 9′ 0″ & 9′ 3″
Seats: 2nd, 76
Weight:
Equipment: Four English Electric 192 h.p. d.c. traction motors
Nos.: E62431–4

Driving Trailer Open Second (L)

Body: 63′ 11½″×9′ 0″ & 9′ 3″
Seats: 2nd, 80
Weight: 36 tons
Nos.: E75920–3

313	315	316
314		

Class 308/2 Fenchurch St.-Shoeburyness Four-Car Units

B.R. Standard design
Introduced: 1961

Driving Trailer Second

Body: 63′ 11½″×9′ 0″ & 9′ 3″
Seats: 2nd, 108
Weight: 32 tons
Nos.: E75957–61

Trailer Composite (H)

Body: 63′ 6″×9′ 0″ & 9′ 3″
Seats: 1st, 19; **2nd,** 60
Weight: 31 tons
Nos.: E70648–52

Non-Driving Motor Luggage Van

Body: 63′ 6″×9′ 0″ & 9′ 3″
Weight: 51 tons 12 cwt
Equipment: Four English Electric 192 h.p. d.c. traction motors
Nos.: E68012/5–8

Driving Trailer Open Second (L)

Body: 63′ 11½″×9′ 0″ & 9′ 3″
Seats: 2nd, 80
Weight: 36 tons
Nos.: E75924–8

317	319	321
318	320	

Class 305/1 and *308/3 Liverpool St.-Enfield and Chingford Three-Car Units

B.R. Standard design
Introduced: 1960 (*1961)

Driving Trailer Open Second

Body: 63′ 11½″×9′ 0″ & 9′ 3″
Seats: 2nd, 94
Weight:
Nos.: E75462–513, E75741–3

Non-Driving Motor Open Brake Second

Body: 63′ 6″×9′ 0″ & 9′ 3″
Seats: 2nd, 84
Weight:
Equipment: Four G.E.C. 200 h.p. d.c. traction motors
Nos.: E61429–80, E61689–91
*Four English Electric 200 h.p. d.c. traction motors

Driving Trailer Open Second

Body: 63′ 11½″×9′ 0″ & 9′ 3″
Seats: 2nd, 94
Weight:
Nos.: E75514–65, E75992–4

401	420	438
402	421	439
403	422	440
404	423	441
405	424	442
406	425	443
407	426	444
408	427	445
409	428	446
410	429	447
411	430	448
412	431	449
413	432	450
414	433	451
415	434	452
416	435	453*
417	436	454*
418	437	455*
419		

Class 305/2
G.E. Outer Suburban Four-Car Units

B.R. Standard design
Introduced: 1960

Driving Trailer Second

Body: 64′ 0½″ × 9′ 0″ & 9′ 3″
Seats: **2nd**, 108
Weight: 32 tons
Nos.: E75443–61

Trailer Composite (H)

Body: 63′ 6″ × 9′ 0″ & 9′ 3″
Seats: **1st**, 19; **2nd**, 60
Weight: 31 tons
Nos.: E70356–74

Non-Driving Motor Brake Second

Body: 63′ 6″ × 9′ 0″ & 9′ 3″
Seats: **2nd**, 96
Weight: 54 tons
Equipment: Four G.E.C. 200 h.p. d.c. traction motors
Nos.: E61410–28

Driving Trailer Open Second (L)

Body: 64′ 0½″ × 9′ 0″ & 9′ 3″
Seats: **2nd**, 80
Weight: 36 tons
Nos.: E75424–42

501	508	514
502	509	515
503	510	516
504	511	517
505	512	518
506	513	519
507		

Class 309/1
Liverpool St.-Clacton and Walton Two-Car Units

B.R. Standard design
Gangwayed throughout
Introduced: 1962

Motor Brake Second (K)

Body: 64′ 9¾″ × 9′ 0″ & 9′ 3″
Seats: **2nd**, 48
Weight: 59 tons 6 cwt
Equipment: Four G.E.C. 282 h.p. d.c. traction motors
Nos.: E61940–3

Driving Trailer Saloon Second (L)

Body: 64′ 9¾″ × 9′ 0″ & 9′ 3″
Seats: **2nd**, 60
Weight: 39 tons 11 cwt
Nos.: E75984–7

601	603	604
602		

Class 309/4
Liverpool St.-Clacton and Walton Four-Car Units

B.R. Standard design
Gangwayed throughout
Introduced:
As Class 309/1: 1962;
As Class 309/4: 1974.

Motor Brake Second (K)

Body: 64′ 9¾″ × 9′ 0″ & 9′ 3″
Seats: **2nd**, 48
Weight: 59 tons 6 cwt
Equipment: Four G.E.C. 282 h.p. d.c. traction motors
Nos.: E61944–7

Trailer Composite (K)

Body: 64′ 6″ × 9′ 0″ & 9′ 3″
Seats: **1st**, 24; **2nd**, 24
Weight:
Nos.: E71111–4

Trailer Saloon Second (L)

Body: 64′ 6″ × 9′ 0″ & 9′ 3″
Seats: **2nd**, 64
Weight:
Nos.: E71107–10

Class 309/1 2-car unit No. 601 leads a Clacton train at Shenfield [D. Williams

Driving Trailer Saloon Second (L)

Body: 64′ 9¾″ × 9′ 0″ & 9′ 3″
Seats: 2nd, 60
Weight: 39 tons 11 cwt
Nos.: E75988–91

605	607	608
606		

Class 309/2 Liverpool St.-Clacton and Walton Four-Car Buffet Units

B.R. Standard design
Gangwayed throughout
Introduced: 1962

Driving Trailer Composite (H)

Body: 64′ 9¾″ × 9′ 0″ & 9′ 3″
Seats: 1st, 18; **2nd,** 32
Weight: 39 tons 7 cwt
Nos.: E75637–44

Non-Driving Motor Brake Second (K)

Body: 64′ 6″ × 9′ 0″ & 9′ 3″
Seats: 2nd, 48
Weight: 56 tons 16 cwt
Equipment: Four G.E.C. 282 h.p. d.c. traction motors
Nos.: E61932–9

Trailer Griddle/Buffet Car

Body: 64′ 6″ × 9′ 0″ & 9′ 3″
Seats: Buffet, 32
Weight: 35 tons 16 cwt
Nos.: E69100–8

Driving Trailer Saloon Composite (L)

Body: 64′ 9¾″ × 9′ 0″ & 9′ 3″
Seats: 1st, 18; **2nd,** 32
Weight: 36 tons 1 cwt
Nos.: E75976–83

611	614	617
612	615	618
613	616*	

*Unit 616 has an ex-DMU Trailer Buffet Second

Class 309/3 Liverpool St.-Clacton and Walton Four-Car Units

B.R. Standard design
Gangwayed throughout
Introduced: 1962

Driving Trailer Composite (H)

Body: 64′ 9¾″ × 9′ 0″ & 9′ 3″
Seats: 1st, 18; **2nd,** 32
Weight: 39 tons 7 cwt
Nos.: E75962–8

Non-Driving Motor Brake Second (K)

Body: 64′ 6″ × 9′ 0″ & 9′ 3″
Seats: 2nd, 48
Weight: 56 tons 16 cwt
Equipment: Four G.E.C. 282 h.p. d.c. traction motors
Nos.: E61925–31

Trailer Saloon Second (L)

Body: 64′ 6″ × 9′ 0″ & 9′ 3″
Seats: 2nd, 64
Weight: 34 tons 8 cwt
Nos.: E70253–9

Driving Trailer Saloon Composite (H)

Body: 64′ 9¾″ × 9′ 0″ & 9′ 3″
Seats: 1st, 18; **2nd,** 32
Weight: 36 tons 15 cwt
Nos.: E75969–75

621	624	626
622	625	627
623		

Class 313 inner suburban 3-car unit No. 313 004 [*C. N. Rayner*

Class 312/0 GN, 312/1 GE and 312/2 LM Outer Suburban Four-Car Units

B.R. Standard design
Gangwayed within unit
Introduced: 1975

Driving Trailer Open Second (L)

Body: 65′ $1\frac{5}{8}$″ × 9′ 0″ & 9′ 3″
Seats: 2nd, 84
Weight: 34 tons 7 cwt
Nos.: 76949–97

Non-Driving Motor Open Brake Second

Body: 65′ $4\frac{1}{4}$″ × 9′ 0″ & 9′ 3″
Seats: 2nd, 68
Weight: 54 tons 12 cwt
Equipment: Four G.E.C. 270 h.p. d.c. traction motors
Nos.: 62484–528

Trailer Open Second

Body: 65′ $4\frac{1}{4}$″ × 9′ 0″ & 9′ 3″
Seats: 2nd, 98
Weight: 29 tons 17 cwt
Nos.: 71168–212/77–80

Driving Trailer Open Composite (L)

Body: 65′ $1\frac{5}{8}$″ × 9′ 0″ & 9′ 3″
Seats: 1st, 25; **2nd**, 47
Weight: 32 tons 2 cwt
Nos.: 78000–48

Class 312/0

312 001	312 010	312 019
312 002	312 011	312 020
312 003	312 012	312 021
312 004	312 013	312 022
312 005	312 014	312 023
312 006	312 015	312 024
312 007	312 016	312 025
312 008	312 017	312 026
312 009	312 018	

Class 312/1

312 101	312 108	312 114
312 102	312 109	312 116
312 103	312 110	312 117
312 104	312 111	312 115
312 105	312 112	312 118
312 106	312 113	312 119
312 107		

Class 312/2

312 201	312 203	312 204
312 202		

Class 313 GN Inner Suburban Three-Car Units

B.R. Standard design with air-operated sliding doors
Gangwayed throughout
(These units are also equipped to work from 750 V. d.c. 3rd rail in tunnel sections)
Introduced: 1976

Motor Open Brake Second

Body: 64′ $11\frac{1}{2}$″ × 9′ 3″
Seats: 2nd, 74
Weight: 35.94 tonnes
Equipment: Four 110 h.p. G.E.C. traction motors
Nos.: 62529–92

Trailer Open Second

Body: 65′ $4\frac{1}{4}$″ × 9′ 3″
Seats: 2nd, 84
Weight: 31.76 tonnes
Nos.: 71213–76

Motor Open Brake Second

Body: 64′ $11\frac{1}{2}$″ × 9′ 3″
Seats: 2nd, 74
Weight: 37.74 tonnes
Equipment: Four 110 h.p. G.E.C. traction motors
Nos.: 62593–628

313 001	313 023	313 044
313 002	313 024	313 045
313 003	313 025	313 046
313 004	313 026	313 047
313 005	313 027	313 048
313 006	313 028	313 049
313 007	313 029	313 050
313 008	313 030	313 051
313 009	313 031	313 052
313 010	313 032	313 053
313 011	313 033	313 054
313 012	313 034	313 055
313 013	313 035	313 056
313 014	313 036	313 057
313 015	313 037	313 058
313 016	313 038	313 059
313 017	313 039	313 060
313 018	313 040	313 061
313 019	313 041	313 062
313 020	313 042	313 063
313 021	313 043	313 064
313 022		

Class 315 GE Liverpool St.-Shenfield Inner Suburban Four-Car Units

B.R. Standard design with air-operated sliding doors
Gangwayed throughout
To be introduced:

Motor open Brake Second

Body:
Seats: 2nd, 74
Weight:
Equipment:

Non Driving Motor Open Second

Body:
Seats: 2nd, 84
Weight:
Equipment:

Trailer Open Second

Body:
Seats: 2nd, 84
Weight:

Driving Trailer Open Brake Second

Body:
Seats: 2nd, 74
Weight:

315 001	315 022	315 042
315 002	315 023	315 043
315 003	315 024	315 044
315 004	315 025	315 045
315 005	315 026	315 046
315 006	315 027	315 047
315 007	315 028	315 048
315 008	315 029	315 049
315 009	315 030	315 050
315 010	315 031	315 051
315 011	315 032	315 052
315 012	315 033	315 053
315 013	315 034	315 054
315 014	315 035	315 055
315 015	315 036	315 056
315 016	315 037	315 057
315 017	315 038	315 058
315 018	315 039	315 059
315 019	315 040	315 060
315 020	315 041	315 061
315 021		

Class 920 Prototype Suburban Three-Car Unit

B.R. Standard design with air-operated sliding doors
Gangwayed throughout
Introduced: 1975

Motor Open Brake Second

Body: 64′ 11½″ × 9′ 3″
Seats: 2nd
Weight:
Equipment: Four 100 h.p. English Electric traction motors

Trailer Open Second

Body: 65′ 4¼″ × 9′ 3″
Seats: 2nd
Weight:

Motor Open Brake Second

(As above)

920 001

Southern Region

SYSTEM:
750/850 VOLTS D.C. 3rd RAIL

Class 491
Four-Car Trailer Units (4-TC)

B.R. Standard design
Gangwayed throughout
Introduced: 1966 and 1974*

Driving Trailer Saloon Second

Body: 64′ 6″ × 9′ 0″ & 9′ 3″
Seats: 2nd, 64
Weight: 32 tons
Nos.: S76270–332, S76943–47

Trailer Brake Second (K)

Body: 64′ 6″ × 9′ 0″ & 9′ 3″
Seats: 2nd, 32
Weight: 35 tons
Nos.: S70812–43, S71160/1

Trailer First (K)

Body: 64′ 6″ × 9′ 0″ & 9′ 3″
Seats: 1st, 42
Weight: 33 tons
Nos.: S70844–71, S71162–7

Driving Trailer Saloon Second

(As above)

401	413	424
402	414	425
403	415	426
404	416	427
405	417	428
406	418	429
407	419	430
408	420	431
409	421	432*
410	422	433*
411	423	434*
412		

Class 430
Four-Car Units (4-REP)

B.R. Standard design
Gangwayed throughout
Introduced: 1967 and 1974*
(These units work in conjunction with 4-TC trailer units and are not normally worked in multiple with other powered units)

Motor Saloon Second

Body: 64′ 6″ × 9′ 0″ & 9′ 3″
Seats: 2nd, 64
Weight: 52 tons
Equipment: Four 365 h.p. English Electric traction motors
Nos.: S62141–62, S62476–83

Trailer Buffet (L)

Body: 64′ 6″ × 9′ 0″ & 9′ 3″
Seats: 19
Weight: 34 tons
Nos.: S69319–29, S69022–5

Trailer Brake First (K)

Body: 64′ 6″ × 9′ 0″ & 9′ 3″
Seats: 1st, 24
Weight: 35 tons
Nos.: S70801–11, S71156–9

Motor Saloon Second

(As above)

3001	3006	3011
3002	3007	3012*
3003	3008	3013*
3004	3009	3014*
3005	3010	3015*

Class 491 4-TC unit No. 411 entering Mortimer [*Marion Canning*

Class 405/2
Four-Car Suburban Units (4-SUB)

Introduced: 1948/9

Motor Open Brake Second

Body: 62′ 6″ × 9′ 0″ & 9′ 3″
Seats: 2nd, 82
Weight: 39 tons
Equipment: Two 250 h.p. English Electric traction motors
Nos.: S10849–58/61–7/9–72/74–8/80–93. 11323/39S

Trailer Second (Trailer Open Second*)

Body: 62′ 0″ × 9′ 0″ & 9′ 3″
Seats: 2nd, 120, (102*)
Weight: 28 tons
Nos.: S10121–5/7/9–35/7–48/50/2/3–8/60–5S, S12374/80S

Trailer Open Second

Body: 62′ 0″ × 9′ 0″ & 9′ 3″
Seats: 2nd, 102
Weight: 28 tons

Motor Open Brake Second

(As Above)

4277*	4285*	4293*
4278	4286	4294*
4279*	4287	4295
4280	4288	4296
4281	4289	4298*
4283	4290	4299*
4284*	4291*	

Class 405/2
Four-Car Suburban Units (4-SUB)

Introduced: 1949/50

Motor Open Brake Second

Body: 62′ 6″ × 9′ 0″ & 9′ 3″
Seats: 2nd, 82
Weight: 39 tons
Equipment: Two 250 h.p. English Electric traction motors
Nos.: Random from S8600S, S11300S and S12600S series

Trailer Open Second (Trailer Second*)

Body: 62′ 0″ × 9′ 0″ & 9′ 3″
Seats: 2nd, 120 (102†, 108‡)
Weight: 28 tons (27 tons‡)
Nos.: Random mainly from S8900S, S10200S and S12300S series

Trailer Open Second

(As above)

Motor Open Brake Second

(As above)

4617	4656	4696
4618	4657	4697*
4619	4658	4701*
4620	4659	4705*
4621	4660*	4709*
4623	4662	4710
4626	4664*	4714*
4627	4666	4716*
4628*	4668	4718
4629*	4669*	4719*
4630*	4670	4721*
4631*	4671	4722
4632*	4672	4725
4633	4673*	4726
4635*	4674	4730
4636*	4675*	4732
4637	4677*	4733
4638*	4678	4735*
4639	4679	4738
4641*	4680	4739
4643*	4681*	4742*
4645	4682	4743
4648*	4683*	4747*
4649	4684*	4749
4650*	4687	4750
4651	4689*	4751*
4653*	4692*	4753*
4654	4693*	4754*
4655*	4695*	

Class 415/1
Four-Car Suburban Units (4-EPB)

Introduced: 1951–4

Motor Open Brake Second (Motor Semi-Open Brake Second‡§■)

Body: 62′ 6″ × 9′ 0″ & 9′ 3″
‡63′ 11½″ × 9′ 0″ & 9′ 3″
Seats: **2nd**, 82 (84‡■)
Weight: 40 tons
Equipment: Two 250 h.p. English Electric traction motors
Nos.: S14001–106S and S14201–465

Trailer Second (Trailer Open Second■)

Body: 62′ 0″ × 9′ 0″ & 9′ 3″
Seats: **2nd**, 120 (108* 102■)
Weight: 28 tons (27 tons■)
Nos.: Random from S15001–S15450S series

Trailer Open Second (Trailer Second†§)

Body: 62′ 0″ × 9′ 0″ & 9′ 3″
Seats: **2nd**, 102 (120†)
Weight: 27 tons (28 tons†)
(Nos. as above)

Motor Open Brake Second (Motor Semi-Open Brake Second§■)

(As above)

5001
5002
5003
5004
5005*
5006
5007
5008*
5009
5010
5011
5012
5013
5014
5015
5016
5017
5018
5019
5020
5021
5022
5024
5025
5026
5027
5028
5029
5030
5031
5032
5033
5034
5035
5036
5037
5038
5039
5040
5041
5042
5043
5044
5045
5046
5048
5049
5050
5051
5052
5053
5101
5102
5104
5105
5106
5107
5108
5109
5110
5111
5112
5113
5114
5115*
5116
5117
5118
5119
5120
5121
5122
5123
5124
5125
5126
5127
5128
5129
5131
5132
5133
5134
5135
5136
5137
5138
5139
5140
5142
5143
5144
5145
5146
5147
5148
5149
5150
5151
5152
5153
5154
5155
5156
5157
5158
5159
5160
5161
5162
5163
5164
5165
5166
5168
5169
5170
5171
5172
5173
5174
5175
5176
5177
5178
5179
5180
5181
5182
5183
5184
5185
5186
5187
5188
5189
5190
5191
5192
5193
5194
5195
5196
5197
5198
5199
5200
5201
5202
5203
5205
5206
5207
5208
5209
5210
5211
5212
5213
5214
5215
5216
5217
5218
5219
5220
5221
5222
5223
5224
5225
5226
5227
5228
5229
5230
5231
5232
5233
5234

Class 430 4-REP unit No. 3006 passing Clapham Junction [*B. Morrison*

Class 405/2 4-SUB unit No. 4678 [*B. Morrison*

Class 415/2 4-EPB unit No. 5327 on a Charing Cross–Sevenoaks working [B. Morrison

5235	5245†	5255
5236	5246‡	5256
5237	5247	5257
5238	5248	5258
5239	5249	5259
5240	5250	5260
5241	5251	5261§
5242	5252	5262‡
5243	5253	5263■
5244	5254	5264■

*Units 5005/8, 5115, 5220 have one nine-compartment trailer second
†Unit 5245 has two trailer compartment seconds
‡Units 5246/62 have one BR standard motor coach
§Unit 5261 has two BR standard motor coaches and two trailer compartment seconds
■ Units 5263/4 have two trailer open seconds

Class 415/2 Four-Car Suburban Units (4-EPB)

Motor coaches only: B.R. Standard design
Introduced: 1960

Motor Semi-Open Brake Second

Body: 63′ 11½″×9′ 0″ & 9′ 3″
Seats: 2nd, 84
Weight: 40 tons
Equipment: Two 250 h.p. English Electric traction motors
Nos.: S61625–7/S65308S

Trailer Second

Body: 62′ 0″×9′ 0″ & 9′ 3″
Seats: 2nd, 120
Weight: 28 tons
Nos.: S15043/79S

Trailer Open Second

Body: 62′ 0″×9′ 0″ & 9′ 3″
Seats: 2nd, 102 (120*)
Weight: 27 tons
Nos.: S15121/413S

Motor Semi-Open Brake Second

(As above)

5301	5302

Class 415/2 Four-Car Suburban Units (4-EPB)

B.R. Standard design
Introduced: 1960–4

Motor Semi-Open Brake Second

Body: 63′ 11½″×9′ 0″ & 9′ 3″
Seats: 2nd, 84
Weight: 39 tons or 40 tons
Equipment: Two 250 h.p. English Electric traction motors
Nos.: S61516–S61623, S61989–S62016

Trailer Semi-Compartment Second

Body: 63′ 6″×9′ 0″ & 9′ 3″
Seats: 2nd, 112
Weight: 29 tons
Nos.: S70375–482, S70667–94

Trailer Semi-Compartment Second

(As above)

Motor Semi-Open Brake Second

(As above)

5303*	5311*	5319*
5304*	5312*	5320
5305*	5313*	5321
5306	5314*	5322
5307*	5315*	5323
5308*	5316	5324
5309*	5317*	5325
5310*	5318*	5326

Class 415/1 4-EPB unit No. 5184 near Elmstead Woods [B. Morrison

5327	5342	5357
5328	5343	5358
5329	5344	5359
5330	5345	5360
5331	5346	5361
5332	5347	5362
5333	5348	5363
5334	5349	5364
5335	5350	5365
5336	5351	5366
5337	5352	5367
5338	5353	5368
5339	5354	5369
5340	5355	5370
5341	5356	

*Fitted with express gear ratio

Class 418/0
Two-Car Units (2-SAP)

Introduced: as Class 414: 1958; as Class 418: 1976

Motor Semi-Open Brake Second (Motor Open Brake Second*)

Body: 62′ 6″×9′ 0″ & 9′ 3″
Seats: 2nd, 84 (82*)
Weight: 40 tons
Equipment: Two 250 h.p. English Electric traction motors
Nos.: S14521–56

Driving Trailer Second (K)

Body: 62′ 6″×9′ 0″ & 9′ 3″
Seats: 2nd, 60
Weight: 32 tons
Nos.: S16001–36

5604	5613	5622
5605	5614	5623
5606	5615	5624*
5607	5616	5625
5608	5617	5626
5609	5618	5627
5610	5619	5628
5611	5620	5629
5612	5621	5630
5631	5633	5635
5632	5634	

*Unit 5624 has an SR-type 4-EPB open motor coach

Class 416/1
Two-Car Suburban Units (2-EPB)

Introduced: 1953–6

Motor Semi-Open Brake Second

Body: 62′ 6″×9′ 0″ & 9′ 3″
Seats: 2nd, 84
Weight: 40 tons
Equipment: Two 250 h.p. English Electric traction motors
Nos.: S14557–90

Driving Trailer Semi-Open Second

Body: 62′ 6″×9′ 0″ & 9′ 3″
Seats: 2nd, 94
Weight: 30 tons
Nos.: S16101–34

5651	5663	5674
5652	5664	5675
5653	5665	5676
5654	5666	5677
5655	5667	5678
5656	5668	5679
5657	5669	5680
5658	5670	5681
5659	5671	5682
5660	5672	5683
5661	5673	5684
5662		

Class 416/2
Two-Car Suburban Units (2-EPB)

B.R. Standard design
Introduced: 1953–6 (*On South Tyneside 1955; modified for SR 1963)

Motor Semi-Open Brake Second

Body: 63′ 11½″×9′ 0″ & 9′ 3″
Seats: 2nd, 84 (74*)
Weight: 40 tons
Equipment: Two 250 h.p. English Electric traction motors
Nos.: S65301–9/11–92

Driving Trailer Semi-Compartment Second

Body: 63′ 11½″×9′ 0″ & 9′ 3″
Seats: 2nd, 102
Weight: 30 tons
Nos.: S77501–78, S77100–14

5702	5736	5765
5703	5737	5767
5705	5738	5768
5706	5739	5769
5707	5740	5770
5710	5741	5771
5712	5742	5772
5713	5743	5773
5714	5744	5774
5715	5745	5775
5716	5746	5776
5717	5747	5777
5718	5748	5778
5719	5749	5779
5720	5750	5781*
5721	5751	5782*
5722	5752	5783*
5723	5753	5784*
5724	5754	5785*
5725	5755	5786*
5726	5756	5787*
5727	5757	5788*
5728	5758	5789*
5729	5759	5790*
5730	5760	5791*
5731	5761	5792*
5732	5762	5793*
5733	5763	5794*
5734	5764	5795*
5735		

Classes 418/1 and 418/2* Two-Car Units (2-SAP)

B.R. Standard design
Introduced: As Class 414: 1957 (1958*); as Class 418: 1974

Motor Semi-Open Brake Second

Body: 63′ 11½″×9′ 0″ & 9′ 3″
Seats: 2nd, 84
Weight: 40 tons
Equipment: Two 250 h.p. English Electric traction motors
Nos.: Mainly S65400 series

Driving Trailer Second (H)

Body: 63′ 11½″×9′ 0″ & 9′ 3″
Seats: 2nd, 75
Weight: 30 tons
Nos.: S77100 series

5901	5918	5935
5902	5919	5936
5903	5920	5937
5904	5921	5938
5905	5922	5939
5906	5923	5940
5907	5924	5941*
5908	5925	5942*
5909	5926	5943*
5910	5927	5944*
5911	5928	5945*
5912	5929	5946*
5913	5930	5947*
5914	5931	5948*
5915	5932	5949*
5916	5933	5950*
5917	5934	

Classes 414/2* and 414/3 Two-Car Units (2-HAP)

B.R. Standard design
Introduced: 1957* (1958–63)

Motor Semi-Open Brake Second

Body: 63′ 11½″×9′ 0″ & 9′ 3″
Seats: 2nd, 84

Class 416/2 2-EPB unit No. 5753 at Merton Park [*J. Scrace*

Class 418/1 2-SAP unit No. 5937 at Staines Moor on a working from Windsor [*C. J. Leigh*

Class 414/3 2-HAP unit No. 6161 *[B. Morrison*

Weight: 40 tons
Equipment: Two 250 h.p. English Electric traction motors
Nos: S61243–303, S61648–88, S61962–88

Driving Trailer Composite (H)

Body: 63′ 11½″×9′ 0″ & 9′ 3″
Seats: 1st, 19; **2nd**, 50
Weight: 30 tons
Nos: S75363–423, S75700–40, S75995–76021

6022*	6088	6125
6023*	6089	6126
6053	6090	6127
6054	6091	6128
6055	6092	6129
6056	6093	6130
6057	6094	6131
6058	6095	6132
6059	6096	6133
6060	6097	6134
6061	6098	6135
6062	6099	6136
6063	6100	6137
6064	6101	6138
6065	6102	6139
6066	6103	6140
6067	6104	6141
6068	6105	6142
6069	6106	6143
6070	6107	6144
6071	6108	6145
6072	6109	6146
6073	6110	6147
6074	6111	6148
6075	6112	6149
6076	6113	6150
6077	6114	6151
6078	6115	6152
6079	6116	6153
6080	6117	6154
6081	6118	6155
6082	6119	6156
6083	6120	6157
6084	6121	6158
6085	6122	6159
6086	6123	6160
6087	6124	6161
6162	6166	6170
6163	6167	6171
6164	6168	6172
6165	6169	6173

Classes 410/1* and 410/2 Four-Car Units (4-BEP)

B.R. Standard design
Gangwayed throughout
Introduced: 1956* (1959)

Motor Saloon Brake Second

Body: 64′ 6″×9′ 0″ & 9′ 3″
Seats: 2nd, 56
Weight: 41 tons (40 tons*)
Equipment: Two 250 h.p. English Electric traction motors
Nos: S61041–4, S61390–408, S61792–811

Trailer Composite (K)

Body: 64′ 6″×9′ 0″ & 9′ 3″
Seats: 1st, 24; **2nd**, 24
Weight: 33 tons (31 tons*)
Nos.: S70041/2, S70346–55, S70601–11

Trailer Buffet

Body: 64′ 6″×9′ 0″ & 9′ 3″
Seats: Buffet, 21
Weight: 36 tons (35 tons*)
Nos.: S69000–21

Motor Saloon Brake Second

(As Above)

7001*	7009	7016
7002*	7010	7017
7003	7011	7018
7004	7012	7019
7005	7013	7020
7006	7014	7021
7007	7015	7022
7008		

Class 410/2 4-BEP unit No. 7020 on "Royal Train" duty at Portsmouth Harbour [B. L. Jackson

Classes 420/1 and 420/2* Four-Car Units (4-BIG)

B.R. Standard design
Gangwayed throughout
Introduced: 1965 (1970*)

Driving Trailer Composite (H)

Body: 64′ 6″×9′ 0″ & 9′ 3″
Seats: 1st, 24; **2nd,** 28
Weight:
Nos.: S76058–75, S76571–5/7–80

Trailer Buffet

Body: 64′ 6″×9′ 0″ & 9′ 3″
Seats: 2nd, 40
Weight:
Nos.: S69301–18, S69330–9

Non-Driving Motor Saloon Brake Second

Body: 64′ 6″×9′ 0″ & 9′ 3″
Seats: 2nd, 56
Weight:
Equipment: Four 250 h.p. English Electric traction motors
Nos.: S62053–70, S62277–86

Driving Trailer Composite (H)

Body: 64′ 6″×9′ 0″ & 9′ 8″
Seats: 1st, 18; **2nd,** 36
Weight:
Nos.: S76112–29, S76561–5/7–70

7031	7041	7050*
7032	7042	7051*
7033	7043	7052*
7034	7044	7053*
7035	7045	7054*
7036	7046	7055*
7037	7047	7056*
7038	7048	7057*
7039	7049*	7058*
7040		

Classes 411/1*, 411/2 and 411/3‡ Four-Car Units (4-CEP)

B.R. Standard design
Gangwayed throughout
Introduced: 1956*, 1958–63 (rebuilt 1975‡)

Motor Saloon Brake Second (Motor Saloon Second‡)

Body: 64′ 6″×9′ 0″ & 9′ 3″
Seats: 2nd, 56 (64‡)
Weight: 41 tons (40 tons*)
Equipment: Two 250 h.p. English Electric traction motors
Nos.: S61033–40, S61229–389, S61695–790, S61868/9, 61948–60

Trailer Composite (K) (Trailer Brake Composite (K)‡)

Body: 64′ 6″×9′ 0″ & 9′ 3″
Seats: 1st, 24 (24‡), **2nd,** 24 (6‡)
Weight: 33 tons (31 tons*)
Nos.: S70037–40, S70235–40, S70303–45, S70552–70600, S70653–9

Trailer Second (K) (Trailer Saloon Second (L) ‡)

Body: 64′ 6″×9′ 0″ & 9′ 3″
Seats: 2nd, 64 (†56)
Weight: 32 tons (31 tons*)
Nos.: S70033–6, S70229–34, S70260–70302, S70503–51, S70660–66

Motor Saloon Brake Second (Motor Saloon Second‡)

(As Above)

7101*	7110	7118
7103*	7111	7119
7104*	7112	7120
7105	7113	7121
7106	7114	7122
7107	7115	7123
7108	7116	7124
7109	7117	7125

7126	7154	7183
7127	7155	7184
7128	7156	7185
7129	7157	7186
7130	7158	7187
7131	7159	7188
7132	7160	7189†
7133	7161	7190
7134	7162	7191
7135	7163	7192
7136	7164	7193
7137	7165	7194
7138	7166	7195
7139	7167	7196
7140	7168	7197
7141	7169	7198
7142	7170	7199
7143	7171	7200
7144	7172	7201
7145	7173	7202
7146	7174	7203
7147	7175	7205
7148	7176	7206
7149	7177	7207
7150	7178	7208
7151	7179	7209
7152	7180	7210
7153‡	7182	7211

Classes 421/1* and 421/2 Four-Car Units (4-CIG)

B.R. Standard design
Gangwayed throughout
Introduced: 1964*, 1970–2

Driving Trailer Composite (H)

Body: 64′ 6″×9′ 0″ & 9′ 3″
Seats: 1st, 24; **2nd**, 28
Weight:
Nos.: S76022–57, S76611–40, S76788–860

Trailer Saloon Second

Body: 64′ 6″×9′ 0″ & 9′ 3″
Seats: 2nd, 72
Weight:
Nos.: S70695–70730, S70967–96, S71035–71106

Non-Driving Motor Saloon Brake Second

Body: 64′ 6″×9′ 0″ & 9′ 3″
Seats: 2nd, 56
Weight:
Equipment: Four 250 h.p. English Electric traction motors
Nos.: S62017–52, S62287–316, S62355–425

Driving Trailer Composite (H)

Body: 64′ 6″×9′ 0″ & 9′ 3″
Seats: 1st, 18; **2nd**, 36
Weight:
Nos.: S76076–111, S76581–610, S76717–76787

7301*	7329*	7357
7302*	7330*	7358
7303*	7331*	7359
7304*	7332*	7360
7305*	7333*	7361
7306*	7334*	7362
7307*	7335*	7363
7308*	7336*	7364
7309*	7337	7365
7310*	7338	7366
7311*	7339	7367
7312*	7340	7368
7313*	7341	7369
7314*	7342	7370
7315*	7343	7371
7316*	7344	7372
7317*	7345	7373
7318*	7346	7374
7319*	7347	7375
7320*	7348	7376
7321*	7349	7377
7322*	7350	7378
7323*	7351	7379
7324*	7352	7380
7325*	7353	7381
7326*	7354	7382
7327*	7355	7383
7328*	7356	7384

Class 411/2 4-CEP unit No. 7121 at Fratton [*J. Scrace*

Class 421/2 4-CIG unit No. 7421 [*J. Scrace*

Class 423 4-VEP unit No. 7834 leaving Haslemere [*K. Lane*

7385	7403	7421
7386	7404	7422
7387	7405	7423
7388	7406	7424
7389	7407	7425
7390	7408	7426
7391	7409	7427
7392	7410	7428
7393	7411	7429
7394	7412	7430
7395	7413	7431
7396	7414	7432
7397	7415	7433
7398	7416	7434
7399	7417	7435
7400	7418	7436
7401	7419	7437
7402	7420	7438

Class 423 Four-Car Units (4-VEP)

B.R. Standard design
Gangwayed throughout
Introduced: 1967–74

Driving Trailer Composite (H)

Body: 64′ 6″×9′ 0″ & 9′ 3″
Seats: 1st, 24; **2nd,** 38 (30*)
Weight: 34 tons
Nos.: S76230–474, S76475–560, S76642–715, 76862–942

Trailer Open Second

Body: 64′ 6″×9′ 0″ & 9′ 3″
Seats: 2nd, 98 (78*)
Weight: 31 tons
Nos.: S70781–800, S70872–966, S70997–71034, S71115–55

Non-Driving Motor Open Brake Second

Body: 64′ 6″×9′ 0″ & 9′ 3″
Seats: 2nd, 58 (46*)
Weight: 48 tons
Equipment: Four 250 h.p. English Electric traction motors
Nos.: S62121–40, S62182–223, S62224–76, S62317–354, S62435–75

Driving Trailer Composite (H)
(As Above)

7701	7749	7796
7702	7750	7797
7703	7751	7798
7704	7752	7799
7705	7753	7800
7706	7754	7801
7707	7755*	7802
7708	7756	7803
7709	7757	7804
7710	7758	7805
7711	7759	7806
7712	7760	7807
7713	7761	7808
7714	7762	7809
7715	7763	7810
7716	7764	7811
7717	7765	7812
7718	7766	7813
7719	7767	7814
7720	7768	7815
7721	7769	7816
7722	7770	7817
7723	7771	7818
7724	7772	7819
7725	7773	7820
7726	7774	7821
7727	7775	7822
7728	7776	7823
7729	7777	7824
7730	7778	7825
7731	7779	7826
7732	7780	7827
7733	7781	7828
7734	7782	7829
7735	7783	7830
7736	7784	7831
7737	7785	7832
7738	7786	7833
7740	7787	7834
7741	7788	7835
7742	7789	7836
7743	7790	7837
7744	7791	7838
7745	7792	7839
7746	7793	7840
7747	7794	7841
7748	7795	7842

7843	7861	7878
7844	7862	7879
7845	7863	7880
7846	7864	7881
7847	7865	7882
7848	7866	7883
7849	7867	7884
7850	7868	7885
7851	7869	7886
7852	7870	7887
7853	7871	7888
7854	7872	7889
7855	7873	7890
7856	7874	7891
7857	7875	7892
7858	7876	7893
7859	7877	7894
7860		

*Unit 7755 has been experimentally fitted with additional luggage racks in place of certain seats for use on Gatwick Airport Services.

Two-Car Departmental De-Icing Units

(Gangwayed within set)
Introduced: 1967. Converted from 2-HAL motor coaches

Motor Brake De-Icing Van

Body: 62′ 6″×9′ 0″ & 9′ 3″
Weight: 47 tons
Equipment: Two 250 h.p. English Electric traction motors

Motor-Brake De-Icing Van

(As Above)

001 002 003

Introduced: 1977. Converted from 4-SUB motor coaches

004 005 006

Two-Car Departmental De-Icing Units

(Gangwayed within set)
Introduced: 1959

Motor Brake De-Icing Van

Body: 62′ 6″×8′ 6″ & 9′ 0″
Equipment: Two 275 h.p. English Electric traction motors
Weight:

Motor Brake De-Icing Van

(As Above)

011 015 018
013 016 020
014

Two-Car Departmental Stores Units

Introduced: 1970 (1972*)

Motor Brake Stores Van

Body: 62′ 6″×9′ 0″ & 9′ 3″
Equipment: Two 275 h.p. English Electric traction motors
Weight:

Motor Brake Stores Van

(As Above)

022 023 024*

Class 486 Isle of Wight Three-Car Units (3-TIS)

(Ex-London Transport tube size vehicles with air-operated sliding doors). Refurbished 1967 for BR use

Motor Open Brake Second

Body:
Seats: 2nd, 26
Weight: 29 tons
Equipment: Two 240 h.p. traction motors
Nos.: S1/3/5/7/11S

Trailer Open Second

Body:
Seats: 2nd, 42
Weight: 18 tons 10 cwt
Nos.: S47/92–4/96S

Class 486 3-TIS unit No. 034 at Shanklin [*R. E. Ruffell*

Two-car departmental de-icing unit No. 019 [*J. Scrace*

Driving Trailer Open Second
Body:
Seats: 2nd, 38
Weight: 17 tons
Nos.: S26/8/30/2/6S

031	033	035
032	034	

Class 485 Isle of Wight Four-Car Units (4-VEC)
(Ex-London Transport tube size vehicles with air-operated sliding doors. Refurbished in 1967 for BR use)

Motor Open Brake Second
Body:
Seats: 2nd, 26
Weight: 29 tons
Equipment: Two 240 h.p. traction motors
Nos.: S2/4/6/8/9/10/13/15/19–23S

Trailer Open Second
Body:
Seats: 2nd, 38 or 42
Weight: 17 tons or 18 tons 10 cwt
Nos.: S27/9/31/3/4/41–4/6/9/95S

Trailer open Second
(As Above)

Motor Open Brake Second
(As Above)

041	043*	045
042	044	046

*Fitted with de-icing equipment

Four-Car Departmental Instruction Unit
Gangwayed within set
Introduced: 1974
(Formed of stock from withdrawn 4-SUB No. 4367 fitted internally for use as a mobile instruction train)

Motor Brake
Body: 62′ 6″ × 9′ 0″ & 9′ 3″
Weight: 43 tons
Equipment: Two 275 h.p. English Electric traction motors

Trailer
Body: 62′ 0″ × 9′ 0″ & 9′ 3″
Weight: 28 tons

Trailer
(As Above)

Motor Brake
(As Above)

055

Class 419 Single Units
Introduced: 1959–61

Motor Luggage Van
Body: 64′ 6″ × 9′ 0″ & 9′ 3″
Weight: 45 tons
Equipment: Two 250 h.p. English Electric traction motors

(These vehicles can work singly, hauling a limited load, or in multiple with EP-type stock. They are equipped with traction batteries for working on non-electrified quay lines at Dover and Folkstone)

Coach Nos

S68001	S68005	S68008
S68002	S68006	S68009
S68003	S68007	S68010
S68004		

Trailer Departmental De-Icing Vans

(Withdrawn 4-SUB post-war all-steel trailers fitted with conductor rail scraping and spraying equipment; wired for multiple-unit operation with EP-type stock)

Trailer De-Icing Van

Body: 62′ 0″ × 9′ 0″ & 9′ 3″
Weight:

Coach Nos

ADS70050	ADS70086
ADS70051	ADS70087

Single Unit

General Manager's Saloon Trailer

Body: 64′ 6″ × 8′ 2½″ & 9′ 0″
Weight:

(Double-ended driving trailer rebuilt from Hastings line diesel buffet car; may be used with both multiple-unit stock and locomotives)

Coach No.
DB975025

Single Unit

Experimental Driving Trailer

Body: 64′ 6″ × 9′ 0″ & 9′ 3″
Weight:

(Single-ended driving trailer converted from 4-VEP driving trailer composite)

Coach No.
DB975081 Hermes

Test Unit

Former Class 501 driving trailer open brake second converted to mobile laboratory
Previous No. M75165
ADB975032
Currently running with S61035 and S62395 from 4-CEP unit No. 7102

Class 487
Waterloo and City One- or Five-Car Units

(Tube size vehicles with air-operated sliding doors. Trains are formed of a single motor car or up to five-car units comprising two motor cars and three trailers)
Introduced: 1940

Motor Open Brake Second

Body: 47′ 0″ × 8′ 7¾″
Seats: 2nd, 40
Weight:
Equipment: Two 190 h.p. English Electric traction motors

Coach Nos.

51	55	59
52	56	60
53	57	61
54	58	62

Trailer Open Second

Body: 47′ 0″ × 8′ 7¾″
Seats: 2nd, 52
Weight: 18 tons 14 cwt

Coach Nos.

71	77	82
72	78	83
73	79	84
74	80	85
75	81	86
76		

PRESERVED ELECTRIC MULTIPLE-UNITS

Class 401
Two-Car Unit (2-BIL)

Introduced: 1937

Motor Brake Second (K)

Body: 62′ 6″×9′ 0″ & 9′ 3″
Seats: 2nd, 52
Weight: 43 tons 10 cwt
Equipment: Two 275 h.p. English Electric traction motors

Driving Trailer Composite (K)

Body: 62′ 6″×9′ 0″ & 9′ 3″
Seats: 1st, 24; **2nd,** 32
Weight: 31 tons 5 cwt

2090

To be preserved at York Railway Museum

Class 404/2
Four-Car Unit (4-COR)

Gangwayed throughout
Introduced: 1937

Motor Saloon Brake Second

Body: 63′ 6″×9′ 0″ & 9′ 4½″
Seats: 2nd, 52
Weight: 46 tons 10 cwt
Equipment: Two 225 h.p. English Electric traction motors

Trailer Second (K)

Body: 63′ 6″×9′ 0″ & 9′ 3″
Seats: 2nd, 68
Weight: 32 tons 13 cwt

Trailer Composite (K)

Body: 63′ 6″×9′ 0″ & 9′ 3″
Seats: 1st, 30; **2nd,** 24
Weight: 32 tons 12 cwt

Motor Saloon Brake Second

(As Above)

3142

(Preserved by the Southern Electric Group on the Nene Valley Railway, Peterborough)

Four-Car Double-Deck Suburban Unit (4-DD)

Introduced: 1949

Motor Brake Second

Body: 62′ 6″×9′ 0″ & 9′ 3″
Seats: 2nd, lower deck 55, upper deck 55 plus 10 tip-up
Weight: 39 tons
Equipment: Two 250 hp English Electric traction motors

Trailer Second

Body: 62′ 6″×9′ 0″ & 9′ 3″
Seats: 2nd, lower deck 78, upper deck 66 plus 12 tip-up
Weight: 28 tons

Trailer Second

(As above)

Motor Brake Second

(As above)

4902

PRESERVED LOCOMOTIVES

(Section compiled by H. C. Casserley)

Although most preserved locomotives will eventually fall into two groups—preservation by BR or other official body, and preservation by a Society or Trust—the present situation is necessarily complex, with locomotives existing under various categories. They may be already on display or awaiting removal to a museum, stored by BR pending restoration, in use on privately-owned lines, privately-owned (in some cases on behalf of a preservation fund), or stored on BR awaiting completion of purchase or removal to a permanent home, to name but few. Secondly, the locomotives may be in regular or occasional use, capable of being steamed, or totally inactive. Thirdly, they may have reached the preservation stage after service with British Railways, withdrawal for preservation before 1948, or private use (having been sold prior to Nationalisation).

The general principle behind compilation of this section is to give full details of all locomotives and other motive power which ran in regular service on British Railways. Among those included, therefore, are the GWR 4–4–0 *City of Truro* and the two Scottish "veterans" of LMS Group origin. Certain locomotives withdrawn before 1948 which made brief excursions in recent years—such as the GNR Stirling Single and Ivatt Atlantics—are listed at the end with the rest of the locomotives withdrawn for preservation or sold by the "Big Four" companies before 1948 and now preserved by BR or privately. Some exceptions may be found in the lists—the ex-LMS 0–4–0ST No. 11243 has been included with No. 51218, for example—but in these cases, an explanation is given in the class headings.

Locomotives are listed in order of their final BR numbers (shown in brackets where renumbering has subsequently taken place). The number now carried, owner and place of preservation shown are as known at the time of going to press. Where no details of ownership or location are given, the locomotive is generally in store awaiting removal to a permanent site. It should be noted that many preserved locomotives are not available for public inspection; those in museums and at privately-owned railways may be seen at normal viewing times or operating days, however, and certain other locations are open on special occasions.

Corris Railway 0-4-2ST

*Introduced 1878. Falcon Engine and Car Co. design for use on 2′ 3″ gauge Corris Railway. Built as 0–4–0ST but rebuilt by 1901 as 0–4–2ST. Purchased by GWR with railway in 1930.
†Introduced 1921. Kerr Stuart design for Corris Railway. Purchased by GWR with railway in 1930.
Both sold to the Talyllyn Railway, 1948 and still in service.

Weight: *9 tons, †8 tons
Boiler pressure: 160lb/sq in NS
Cylinders: (O) 7″×12″
Driving wheel diameter: 2′ 6″, †2′ 0″
Tractive effort: *2,665 lb, †3,330 lb
Valve gear: Stephenson (slide valves)
†Modified Hackworth (slide valves)

*3 Sir Haydn †4 Edward Thomas

V of R 2-6-2T

Introduced 1902. Davies and Metcalfe design for Vale of Rheidol 1′ 11½″ gauge railway.
*Introduced 1923. GWR development of Vale of Rheidol design.
The only steam locomotives in service with British Railways, operating during the summer on the Aberystwyth–Devil's Bridge Vale of Rheidol line.

Weight: 25 tons
Boiler pressure: 165 lb sq in NS
Cylinders:
(O) 11″×17″, *(O) 11½″×17″
Driving wheel diameter: 2′ 6″
Tractive effort: 9,615 lb, *10,510 lb
Valve gear: Walschaerts (piston valves)

*7 Owain Glyndwr *8 Llywelyn
9 Prince of Wales

W & L 0-6-0T

Introduced 1902. Beyer-Peacock design for Cambrian Railways Welshpool & Llanfair Section 2′ 6″ gauge railway.
In service on the Welshpool & Llanfair Railway.

Weight: 19 tons 18 cwt
Boiler Pressure: 150 lb/sq in NS
Cylinders: (O) 11½″×16″
Driving wheel diameter: 2′ 9″
Tractive effort: 8,175 lb
Valve gear: Walschaerts (slide valves)

1 (822) The Earl
2 (823) The Countess

Cardiff Railway 0-4-0ST

Introduced 1898. Kitson design for Cardiff Railway.
Preserved at Somerset Railway Museum, Bleadon and Uphill Station, but may be moved to Didcot.

Weight: 25 tons 10 cwt
Boiler pressure: 160 lb/sq in NS
Cylinders: (O) 14″×21″
Driving wheel diameter: 3′ 2½″
Tractive effort: 14,540 lb
Valve gear: Hawthorn-Kitson

1338

Class 1361 0-6-0ST

Introduced 1910. Churchward GWR design for dock shunting.
Preserved by the Great Western Society. Didcot.

Weight: 35 tons 4 cwt
Boiler pressure: 150 lb/sq in NS
Cylinders: (O) 16″×20″
Driving wheel diameter: 3′ 8″
Tractive effort: 14,835 lb
Valve gear: Stephenson (slide valves)

1363

BR Vale of Rheidol 2-6-2T No. 7 Owain Glyndwr [*G. R. Hounsell*

Ex-GWR Class 1400 0-4-2T No. 1420 Bulliver [*B. Morrison*

Class 1366 **0-6-0PT**

Introduced 1934. Collet development of 1361 class.
Preserved by the Dart Valley Railway at Buckfastleigh.

Weight: 35 tons 15 cwt
Boiler pressure: 165 lb/sq in NS
Cylinders: (O) 16″×20″
Driving wheel diameter: 3′ 8″
Tractive effort: 16,320 lb
Valve gear: Stephenson (slide valves)

1369

Class 1400 **0-4-2T**

Introduced 1932. Collett design for light branch work (originally designated 4800). Push-and-pull fitted.
[1]Preserved at the Dart Valley Railway, Buckfastleigh.
[2]Preserved on a plinth at Tiverton.
[3]Preserved by the Great Western Society, Didcot.

Weight: 41 tons 6 cwt
Boiler pressure: 165 lb/sq in NS
Cylinders: (I) 16″×24″
Driving wheel diameter: 5′ 2″
Tractive effort: 13,900 lb
Valve gear: Stephenson (slide valves)

1420 Bulliver[1] 1450 Ashburton[1]
1442[2] 1466[3]

Class 1500 **0-6-0PT**

Introduced 1949. Hawksworth short-wheelbase design for heavy shunting.
Preserved by the Warwickshire Railway Society at Bridgnorth.

Weight: 58 tons 4 cwt
Boiler pressure: 200 lb/sq in NS
Cylinders: (O) 17½″×24″
Driving wheel diameter: 4′ 7½″
Tractive effort: 22,515 lb
Valve gear: Walschaerts (piston valves)

1501

Class 1600 **0-6-0PT**

Introduced 1949. Hawksworth light branch line and shunting design.
Preserved at the Dart Valley Railway, Buckfastleigh.

Weight: 41 tons 12 cwt
Boiler pressure: 165 lb/sq in NS
Cylinders: (I) 16½″×24″
Driving wheel diameter: 4′ 1½″
Tractive effort: 18,515 lb
Valve gear: Stephenson (slide valves)

1638

Class 2301 **0-6-0**

Introduced 1883. Dean GWR design, later fitted with superheater.
Preserved at Swindon Railway Museum.

Weight:
Locomotive: 36 tons 16 cwt
Tender: 34 tons 5 cwt
Boiler pressure: 180 lb/sq in Su
Cylinders: (I) 17″×24″
Driving wheel diameter: 5′ 2″
Tractive effort: 17,120 lb
Valve gear: Stephenson (slide valves)

2516

Class 2800 **2-8-0**

Introduced 1903. Churchward GWR design.
*Introduced 1938. Collett locomotives, with side-window cabs and detail alterations.
[1]Preserved at the National Railway Museum, York.

[2]Preserved by the 2857 Society at the Severn Valley Railway, Bridgnorth.
[3]Preserved by the Great Western Society at Didcot.

Weight:
Locomotive: 75 tons 10 cwt
*76 tons 5 cwt
Tender: 40 tons
Boiler pressure: 225 lb/sq in Su
Cylinders: (0) $18\frac{1}{2}'' \times 30''$
Driving wheel diameter: 4′ $7\frac{1}{2}''$
Tractive effort: 35,380 lb
Valve gear: Stephenson (piston valves)

2818[1]
2857[2]
*3822[3]

Class 2251 0-6-0

Introduced 1930. Collett design. Preserved by the Severn Valley Railway Society, Bridgnorth.

Weight:
Locomotive: 43 tons 8 cwt
Tender: 36 tons 15 cwt
Boiler pressure: 200 lb/sq in Su
Cylinders: (I) $17\frac{1}{2}'' \times 24''$
Driving wheel diameter: 5′ 2″
Tractive effort: 20,155 lb
Valve gear: Stephenson (slide valves)

3205

Class 5700 0-6-0PT

Introduced 1929. Collett design.
*Introduced 1933 with detail alterations and modified cab.
[1]Preserved by the Great Western Society at Didcot.
[2]Preserved at the Severn Valley Railway, Bridgnorth.
[3]Preserved at the Keighley & Worth Valley Railway, Haworth.
[4]Preserved by the Worcester Locomotive Society at H. P. Bulmer Ltd, Hereford.
[5]Preserved by the Quainton Railway Society Ltd at Quainton Road.
[6]Preserved at the Standard Gauge Steam Trust, Tyseley.
[7]Privately preserved at NCB, Maesteg.
[8]Preserved by the Dean Forest Railway Preservation Society at Lydney.

Weight: 47 tons 10 cwt, *49 tons
Boiler pressure: 200 lb/sq in NS
Cylinders: (I) $17\frac{1}{2}'' \times 24''$
Driving wheel diameter: 4′ $7\frac{1}{2}''$
Tractive effort: 22,515 lb
Valve gear: Stephenson (slide valves)

*3650[1]	7715[5]
*3738[1]	7752[6]
5764[2]	7760[6]
L89 (5775)[3]	9600[6]
5786[4]	*9642[7]
7714[2]	9681[8]

Class 3440 4-4-0
"City"

Introduced 1903. Churchward GWR design. Withdrawn in 1931 and preserved at York Railway Museum as No. 3717. Returned to service in 1957 as No. 3440 for work on special trains.
Preserved at Swindon Railway Museum.

Weight:
Locomotive: 55 tons 6 cwt
Tender: 36 tons 15 cwt
Boiler pressure: 200 lb/sq in Su
Cylinders: (I) 18″ × 26″
Driving wheel diameter: 6′ $8\frac{1}{2}''$
Tractive effort: 17,790 lb
Valve gear: Stephenson (slide valves)

3717 (3440) City of Truro

Class 4000 4-6-0 "Star"

Introduced 1907. Churchward GWR design developed from No. 4000, introduced as 4–4–2 No. 40 in 1906. Preserved at Swindon Railway Museum.

Weight:
Locomotive: 75 tons 12 cwt
Tender: 46 tons 14 cwt
Boiler pressure: 225 lb/sq in Su
Cylinders: Four, 15" × 26"
Driving wheel diameter: 6' 8½"
Tractive effort: 27,800 lb
Valve gear: Inside Walschaerts, with rocking shafts (piston valves)

4003 Lode Star

Class 4073 4-6-0 "Castle"

Introduced 1923. Collett design, developed from "Star"
*Fitted with 4-row superheater and double chimney.
[1] Preserved at the Science Museum, London.
[2] Privately preserved at Dampier, Australia.
[3] Preserved at Didcot.
[4] Preserved by 7029 Clun Castle Ltd at Tyseley.

Weight:
Locomotive: 79 tons 17 cwt
Tender: 46 tons 14 cwt
Boiler pressure: 225 lb/sq in Su
Cylinders: Four, 16" × 26"
Driving wheel diameter: 6' 8½"
Tractive effort: 31,625 lb
Valve gear: Inside Walschaerts, with rocking shafts (piston valves)

4073 Caerphilly Castle[1]
4079 Pendennis Castle[2]
5029 Nunney Castle[3]
*5043 Earl of Mount Edgcumbe[4]
5051 Earl Bathurst[3]
5080 Defiant[4]
7027 Thornbury Castle[4]
*7029 Clun Castle[4]

Class 5101 and 6100 2-6-2T

5101. Introduced 1929. Development of Collett 5100 Class.
***6100.** Introduced 1931. Development of Collett 5101 class with increased boiler pressure for London suburban area.
[1] Preserved by the GWR Preservation Group.
[2] Preserved at the Severn Valley Railway, Bridgnorth.
[3] Preserved by the Great Western Society, Didcot.
[4] Preserved at Tyseley.

Weight: 78 tons 9 cwt
Boiler pressure:
220 lb/sq in Su, *225 lb/sq in Su
Cylinders: (O) 18" × 30"
Driving wheel diameter: 5' 8"
Tractive effort: 24,300 lb, *27,340 lb
Valve gear: Stephenson (piston valves)

4110[1]	4150[2]	5164[2]
4141[2]	4160[4]	*6106[3]
4144[3]		

Class 4200 and 5205 2-8-0T

4200. Introduced 1910. Churchward GWR design.
***5205.** Introduced 1923. Development of 4200 Class, with larger cylinders and detail alterations.
[1] Preserved at Swansea Maritime Museum.
[2] Preserved by the Dart Valley Railway.

Weight: 81 tons 12 cwt, *82 tons 2 cwt
Boiler pressure: 200 lb/sq in Su

Ex-GWR Class 6100 2-6-2T No. 6106 [*J. R. Smith*

"Castle" Class 4-6-0 No. 7029 Clun Castle [*P. D. Hawkins*

Cylinders: (O) $18\frac{1}{2}'' \times 30''$
*(O) $19'' \times 30''$
Driving wheel diameter: 4′ $7\frac{1}{2}''$
Tractive effort: 31,450 lb, *33,170 lb
Valve gear: Stephenson (piston valves)

4270[1]
*5239

Class 4500 2-6-2T

Introduced 1906. Churchward GWR development of 4400 class with larger wheels and increased boiler pressure.
*Introduced 1927. Collett 4575 Class, with detail alterations and increased weight.
[1]Preserved at the Dart Valley Railway, Buckfastleigh.
[2]Preserved by the 4566 Preservation Society at the Severn Valley Railway, Bridgnorth.
[3]Preserved by Forest Prairie Fund at Dean Forest Railway, Parkend.
[4]Preserved by the Great Western Society at Didcot.
[5]Preserved on the West Somerset Railway, Williton.

Weight: 57 tons, *61 tons
Boiler pressure: 200 lb/sq in Su
Cylinders: (O) $17'' \times 24''$
Driving wheel diameter: 4′ $7\frac{1}{2}''$
Tractive effort: 21,250 lb
Valve gear: Stephenson (piston valves)

4555 Gladiator[1]
4561[5]
4566[2]
*4588 Warrior[1]
*5521[5]
*5541[3]
*5542[5]
*5572[4]

Class 4900 4-6-0
"Hall"

Introduced 1928. Modified design of Collett rebuild with 6′ 0″ driving wheels of "Saint".
[1]Preserved by the Dumbleton Hall Preservation Society at the Dart Valley Railway.
[2]Preserved by the Severn Valley Railway, Bridgnorth.
[3]Preserved by the Great Western Society at Didcot.
[4]Preserved at the Standard Gauge Steam Trust, Tyseley.

Weight:
Locomotive: 75 tons
Tender: 46 tons 14 cwt
Boiler pressure: 225 lb/sq in Su
Cylinders: (O) $18\frac{1}{2}'' \times 30''$
Driving wheel diameter: 6′ 0″
Tractive effort: 27,275 lb
Valve gear: Stephenson (piston valves)

4920 Dumbleton Hall[1]
4930 Hagley Hall[2]
4942 Maindy Hall[3]
4983 Albert Hall[4]
5900 Hinderton Hall[3]

Class 4300 2-6-0

Introduced 1911. Churchward GWR design.
[1]Preserved by the Great Western Society at Didcot.
[2]Preserved by the Great Western (SVR) Association at the Severn Valley Railway.

Weight:
Locomotive: 62 tons
Tender: 40 tons
Boiler pressure: 200 lb/sq in Su
Cylinders: (O) $18\frac{1}{2}'' \times 30''$
Driving wheel diameter: 5′ 8″
Tractive effort: 25,670 lb
Valve gear: Stephenson (piston valves)

5322[1] 9303 (7325)[2]

Class 5600 0-6-2T

Introduced 1924. Collett design for service in Welsh valleys.
[1] Preserved by the Telford Development Association.
[2] Preserved at Tyseley.
[3] Preserved at Steamtown, Carnforth.
[4] Preserved by the 5668 Fund.
[5] Preserved by the North Yorkshire Moors Railway 6619 Fund at Grosmont.
[6] Preserved by the Great Western Society at Didcot.

Weight: 69 tons 6 cwt
Boiler pressure: 200 lb/sq in Su
Cylinders: (I) 18″ × 26″
Driving wheel diameter: 4′ 7½″
Tractive effort: 25,800 lb
Valve gear: Stephenson (piston valves)

5619[1]	5643[3]	6619[5]
5637[2]	5668[4]	6697[6]

Class 6000 4-6-0 "King"

Introduced 1927. Collett design. Later modified with 4-row superheater and double chimney.
[1] Preserved by BRB; on loan to H. P. Bulmer Ltd, Hereford.
[2] Preserved by the King Preservation Society at Quainton Road.

Weight:
Locomotive: 89 tons
Tender: 46 tons 14 cwt
Boiler pressure: 250 lb/sq in Su
Cylinders: Four, 16¼″ × 28″
Driving wheel diameter: 6′ 6″
Tractive effort: 40,285 lb
Valve gear: Inside Walschaerts, with rocking shafts (piston valves)

6000 King George V[1]
6024 King Edward I[2]

Class 6400 0-6-0PT

Introduced 1932. Collett development of 5400 class for light passenger work, with smaller wheels. Push-and-pull fitted.
[1] Preserved at the West Somerset Railway.
[2] Preserved at the Dart Valley Railway, Buckfastleigh.

Weight: 45 tons 12 cwt
Boiler pressure: 180 lb/sq in NS
Cylinders: (I) 16½″ × 24″
Driving wheel diameter: 4′ 7½″
Tractive effort: 18,010 lb
Valve gear: Stephenson (slide valves)

6412 The Flockton Flyer[1]
6430[2]
6435[2]

Class 6959 4-6-0 "Modified Hall"

Introduced 1944. Hawksworth development of "Hall", with larger superheater, one-piece main frames and plate-framed bogie.
[1] Preserved at Severn Valley Railway, Bridgnorth.
[2] Preserved by the Witherslack Hall Society at the Main Line Steam Trust, Loughborough.
[3] Preserved by the Great Western Society, Didcot.
[4] Preserved by members of Quainton Road Society at Quainton Road.

Weight:
Locomotive: 75 tons 16 cwt
Tender: 46 tons 14 cwt
Boiler pressure: 225 lb/sq in Su
Cylinders: (O) 18½″ × 30″
Driving wheel diameter: 6′ 0″
Tractive effort: 27,275 lb
Valve gear: Stephenson (piston valves)

6960 Raveningham Hall[1]
6989 Wightwick Hall[4]
6990 Witherslack Hall[2]
6998 Burton Agnes Hall[3]

Class 7200 2-8-2T

Introduced 1934. Collett development of Churchward 4200 Class, with extended bunker and additional trailing wheels.
Preserved by the Great Western Society at Didcot.

Weight: 92 tons 2 cwt
Boiler pressure: 200 lb/sq in Su
Cylinders: (O) 19″×30″
Driving wheel diameter: 4′ 7½″
Tractive effort: 33,170 lb
Valve gear: Stephenson (piston valves)

7202

Class 7800 4-6-0 "Manor"

Introduced 1938. Collett design for use on secondary lines, incorporating certain parts of withdrawn 4300 class 2-6-0 locomotives.
[1] Privately preserved at Didcot.
[2] Preserved by the Severn Valley Railway, Bridgnorth.
[3] Preserved by the Cambrian Railways Society at Oswestry.
[4] Preserved by the Dart Valley Railway, Buckfastleigh.

Weight:
Locomotive: 68 tons 18 cwt
Tender: 40 tons
Boiler pressure: 225 lb/sq in Su
Cylinders: (O) 18″×30″
Driving wheel diameter: 5′ 8″
Tractive effort: 27,340 lb
Valve gear: Stephenson (piston valves)

7808 Cookham Manor[1]
7812 Erlestoke Manor[2]
7819 Hinton Manor[2]
7822 Foxcote Manor[3]
7827 Lydham Manor[4]

Class 9000 4-4-0

Introduced 1936. Collett rebuilt incorporating "Duke" class boiler and "Bulldog" class frames for work on secondary lines. Numbered in 3200–28 series until 1946.
Privately preserved at the Bluebell Railway, Sheffield Park.

Weight:
Locomotive: 49 tons
Tender: 36 tons 15 cwt
Boiler pressure: 180 lb/sq in NS
Cylinders: (I) 18″×26″
Driving wheel diameter: 5′ 8″
Tractive effort: 18,955 lb
Valve gear: Stephenson (slide valves)

3217 (9017) Earl of Berkeley

Class 9400 0-6-0PT

Introduced 1947. Hawksworth taper boiler design for heavy shunting.
[1] Preserved at Swindon Railway Museum.
[2] Preserved at Quainton Road.

Weight: 55 tons 7 cwt
Boiler pressure: 200 lb/sq in Su
Cylinders: (I) 17½″×24″
Driving wheel diameter: 4′ 7½″
Tractive effort: 22,515 lb
Valve gear: Stephenson (slide valves)

9400[1] 9466[2]

S.R. Steam Locomotives

Class USA 0-6-0T

Introduced 1942. US. Army Transportation Corps design, purchased by SR 1946 and fitted with modified cab and bunker and other detail alterations for use in Southampton Docks.

[1] Preserved by Southern Railway Locomotive Preservation Co Ltd at the Bluebell Railway, Sheffield Park.
[2] Preserved by Kent & East Sussex Railway Society at Rolvenden.
[3] Preserved by Keighley & Worth Valley Railway, Haworth.

Weight: 46 tons 10 cwt
Boiler pressure: 210 lb sq/in NS
Cylinders: (O) 16½"×24"
Driving wheel diameter: 4' 6"
Tractive effort: 21,600 lb
Valve gear: Walschaerts (piston valves)

30064[1]
22 (30065 DS 237) Maunsell[2]
21 (30070 DS 238) Wainwright[2]
72 (30072)[3]

Class B4 0-4-0T

Introduced 1891. Adams LSWR design for shunting in Southampton Docks.

[1] Preserved by the Bulleid Society Ltd at the Bluebell Railway, Sheffield Park.
[2] Preserved at Bressingham Hall, Diss.

Weight: 33 tons 9 cwt
Boiler pressure: 140 lb/sq in NS
Cylinders: (O) 16"×22"
Driving wheel diameter: 3' 9¾"
Tractive effort: 14,650 lb
Valve gear: Stephenson (slide valves)

30096 Normandy[1]
102 (30102)[2]

Class M7 0-4-4 T

Introduced 1897. Drummond LSWR design.

[1] Preserved at Steamtown, USA.
[2] National Railway Museum York (not on display).

Weight: 60 tons 4 cwt
Boiler pressure: 175 lb/sq in NS
Cylinders: (I) 18½"×26"
Driving wheel diameter: 5' 7"
Tractive effort: 19,755 lb
Valve gear: Stephenson (slide valves)

30053[1] 245 (30245)[2]

Class T9 4-4-0

Introduced 1899. Drummond LSWR design, fitted with superheater and larger cylinders by Urie from 1922. Withdrawn 1962, restored to pre-grouping condition and returned to service for use on special trains. National Railway Museum York (not on display).

Weight:
Locomotive: 51 tons 18 cwt
Tender: 44 tons 17 cwt
Boiler pressure: 175 lb/sq in Su
Cylinders: (I) 19"×26"
Driving wheel diameter: 6' 7"
Tractive effort: 17,675 lb
Valve gear: Stephenson (slide valves)

120 (30120)

Class S15 4-6-0

Introduced 1920. Urie LSWR design; development of N15 class for mixed traffic work.

*Introduced 1936. Maunsell development of the Urie LSWR design with higher boiler pressure, reduced cylinder diameter, modified cab and other detail alterations.

[1]Preserved by the Urie S15 Preservation Group at the Mid-Hants Railway, New Alresford.

[2]Preserved by Essex Locomotive Society at Nene Valley Railway, Peterborough.

Weight:
Locomotive: 79 tons 16 cwt
*79 tons 5 cwt
Tender: 57 tons 16 cwt
*56 tons 8 cwt
Boiler pressure:
180 lb/sq in Su
*200 lb/sq in Su
Cylinders:
(O) 21″ × 28″, *(O) 20½″ × 28″
Driving wheel diameter: 5′ 7″
Tractive effort: 28,200 lb, *29,855 lb
Valve gear: Walschaerts (piston valves)

506 (30506)[1]
*841 (30841) Greene King[2]

Class Q 0-6-0

Introduced 1938. Maunsell design, later fitted with multiple-jet blastpipe and large-diameter chimney.
Preserved by the Maunsell Q Locomotive Preservation Society at motive Preservation Society and may go to the Bluebell Railway.

Weight:
Locomotive: 49 tons 10 cwt
Tender: 40 tons 10 cwt
Boiler pressure: 200 lb/sq in
Cylinders: 19″ × 26″
Driving wheel diameter: 5′ 1″
Tractive effort: 26,160 lb
Valve gear: Stephenson (piston valves)

30541

Class 0415 4-4-2T

Introduced 1882. Adams LSWR design, subsequently reboilered. Sold by LSWR in 1917 but purchased from East Kent Railway by SR in 1946 for use on Lyme Regis branch. Preserved by Bluebell Railway at Sheffield Park.

Weight: 55 tons 2 cwt
Boiler pressure: 160 lb/sq in NS
Cylinders: (O) 17½″ × 24″
Driving wheel diameter: 5′ 7″
Tractive effort: 14,920 lb
Valve gear: Stephenson (slide valves)

488 (30583)

Class 0298 2-4-0WT

Introduced 1874. Beattie LSWR design, rebuilt by Adams 1884–92, Urie 1921/2 and Maunsell 1931–5. Retained for use on Wenford Bridge china clay trains.

[1]Preserved by the Quainton Railway Society Ltd at Quainton Road.

[2]Preserved by BRB; loaned to Steamtown, Carnforth.

Weight: 37 tons 16 cwt
Boiler pressure: 160 lb/sq in NS
Cylinders: (O) 16½″ × 20″
Driving wheel diameter: 5′ 7″
Tractive effort: 11,050 lb
Valve gear: Stephenson (slide valves)

E0314 (30585)[1] 30587[2]

Class N15 4-6-0
"King Arthur"

Introduced 1925. Maunsell development of Urie LSWR design with long-travel valves, increased boiler pressure, smaller firebox, modified

Ex-LSWR Class 0415 4-4-2T No. 488 [*J. Scrace*

Ex-SR Class S15 4-6-0 No. 841 Greene King [*G. R. Mortimer*

cab to suit Eastern Section loading gauge and with bogie tender.
Preserved by BRB being restored by Humberside Locomotive Preservation Group.

Weight:
Locomotive: 80 tons 19 cwt
Tender: 57 tons 11 cwt
Boiler pressure: 200 lb/sq in Su
Cylinders: (O) $20\frac{1}{2}'' \times 28''$
Driving wheel diameter: 6′ 7″
Tractive effort: 25,320 lb
Valve gear: Walschaerts (piston valves)

30777 Sir Lamiel

Class LN 4-6-0
"Lord Nelson"

Introduced 1926. Maunsell design. Fitted with modified cylinders, multiple-jet blastpipe and large-diameter chimney by Bulleid in 1938. Preservation by BRB. On loan to Carnforth.

Weight:
Locomotive: 83 tons 10 cwt
Tender: 57 tons 19 cwt
Boiler pressure: 220 lb/sq in Su
Cylinders: Four, $16\frac{1}{2}'' \times 26''$
Driving wheel diameter: 6′ 7″
Tractive effort: 33, 510 lb
Valve gear: Walschaerts (piston valves)

30850 Lord Nelson

Class V 4-4-0
"Schools"

Introduced 1930. Maunsell design.
[1]National Railway Museum, York (not on display).
[2]Preserved by Steamtown, USA; at present on loan to Cape Breton Steam Railway, Canada.
[3]Preserved at the East Somerset Railway, Cranmore.

Weight:
Locomotive: 67 tons 2 cwt
Tender: 42 tons 8 cwt
Boiler pressure: 220 lb/sq in Su
Cylinders: Three, $16\frac{1}{2}'' \times 26''$
Driving wheel diameter: 6′ 7″
Tractive effort: 25,135 lb
Valve gear: Walschaerts (piston valves)

30925 Cheltenham[1]
30926 Repton[2]
928 (30928) Stowe[3]

Class P 0-6-0T

Introduced 1909. Wainwright SECR design for motor train work, subsequently used for light shunting work.
[1]Preserved by Bluebell Railway at Sheffield Park.
[2]Preserved by Kent & East Sussex Railway Society at Rolvenden.

Weight: 28 tons 10 cwt
Boiler pressure: 160 lb/sq in NS
Cylinders: (I) $12'' \times 18''$
Driving wheel diameter: 3′ 9″
Tractive effort: 7,810 lb
Valve gear: Stephenson (slide valves)

27 (31027)[1]
1178 (31178)[1]
323 (31323) Bluebell[1]
11 (31556) Pride of Sussex[2]

Class O1 0-6-0

Introduced 1903. Wainwright rebuild with domed boiler and new cab of Stirling SER O Class.
Privately preserved.

Ex-LBSCR Class A1x 0-6-0T No. 46 Newington [*J. Scrace*

Ex-LSWR Class 02 0-4-4T No. 24 Calbourne [*P. J. Relf*

Weight:
Locomotive: 41 tons 1 cwt
Tender: 28 tons 5 cwt
Boiler pressure: 150 lb/sq in NS
Cylinders: (I) 18"×26"
Driving wheel diameter: 5' 2"
Tractive effort: 17,325 lb
Valve gear: Stephenson (slide valves)

65 (31065)

Class H 0-4-4T

Introduced 1904. Wainwright SECR design.
Preserved by H Class Trust at the Bluebell Railway, Sheffield Park.

Weight: 54 tons 8 cwt
Boiler pressure: 160 lb/sq in NS
Cylinders: (I) 18"×26"
Driving wheel diameter: 5' 6"
Tractive effort: 17,360 lb
Valve gear: Stephenson (slide valves)

263 (31263)

Class C 0-6-0

Introduced 1900. Wainwright SECR design.
Preserved by Wainwright C Preservation Society at the Bluebell Railway, Sheffield Park.

Weight:
Locomotive: 43 tons 16 cwt
Tender: 38 tons 5 cwt
Boiler pressure: 160 lb/sq in NS
Cylinders: (I) 18½"×26"
Driving wheel diameter: 5' 2"
Tractive effort: 19,520 lb
Valve gear: Stephenson (slide valves)

592 (31592)

Class U 2-6-0

Introduced 1928. Maunsell rebuild of SECR K (River) class 2–6–4T.
*New locomotive to same basic design as rebuild, but with detail alterations.
[1] Preserved by the Southern Mogul Preservation Society at Bluebell Railway, Sheffield Park.
[2] Preserved by the Mid-Hants Railway Preservation Society at New Alresford.

Weight:
Locomotive: 63 tons
*62 tons 6 cwt
Tender: 40 tons 10 cwt
*42 tons 8 cwt
Boiler Pressure: 200 lb/sq in Su
Cylinders: (O) 19"×28"
Driving wheel diameter: 6' 0"
Tractive effort: 23,865 lb
Valve gear: Walschaerts (piston valves)

*31618[1]　31806[2]

Class D 4-4-0

Introduced 1901. Wainwright SECR design with round-top firebox. Preserved at the National Railway Museum, York.

Weight:
Locomotive: 50 tons
Tender: 39 tons 2 cwt
Boiler pressure: 175 lb/sq in NS
Cylinders: (I) 19"×26"
Driving wheel diameter: 6' 8"
Tractive effort: 17,450 lb
Valve gear: Stephenson (slide valves)

737 (31737)

Class N 2-6-0

Introduced 1917. Maunsell SECR mixed traffic design.

Preserved by the Mid-Hants Railway Preservation Society at New Alresford.

Weight:
Locomotive: 61 tons 4 cwt
Tender: 39 tons 5 cwt
Boiler pressure: 200 lb/sq in Su
Cylinders: (O) 19″×28″
Driving wheel diameter: 5′ 6″
Tractive effort: 26,035 lb
Valve gear: Walschaerts (piston valves)

31874 Aznar Line

Class E4 0-6-2T

Introduced 1897. R. J. Billinton LBSCR design, development of earlier E3 with larger wheels. Fitted with Marsh boiler and extended smokebox in 1910. Cylinder diameter reduced from 18″ by SR.
Preserved by Bluebell Railway at Sheffield Park.

Weight: 57 tons 10 cwt
Boiler pressure: 170 lb/sq in NS
Cylinders: (I) $17\frac{1}{2}$″×26″
Driving wheel diameter: 5′ 6″
Tractive effort: 19,175 lb
Valve gear: Stephenson (slide valves)

473 (32473) Birch Grove

Class A1 and A1X 0-6-0T "Terrier"

***A1.** Introduced 1872. Stroudley LBSCR "Terrier" for suburban work.
●**A1.** Subsequently fitted with Marsh A1X-type boiler but retaining original smoke-box and other details.
†**A1X.** Introduced 1911. Marsh rebuild of A1 with new boiler and extended smokebox.
‡**A1X.** Locomotive with increased cylinder diameter.
§**A1X.** Transferred to the Isle of Wight by SR but returned to mainland for further use in 1949.
¶**A1X.** Locomotive acquired by BR from Kent & East Sussex Railway on Nationalisation.
[1]Preserved at the National Railway Museum, York.
[2]Preserved by Bluebell Railway at Sheffield Park.
[3]Preserved by Wight Locomotive Society at Havenstreet.
[4]Preserved at "Hayling Billy" public house, Hayling Island.
[5]Preserved by Borough of Sutton but on loan to Kent & East Sussex Railway Society at Rolvenden.
[6]Preserved at Bressingham Hall, Diss.
[7]Preserved by Kent & East Sussex Railway Society at Rolvenden.
[8]Preserved at Williton, West Somerset Railway.
[9]Preserved at Montreal Railway Historical Museum, Canada.

Weight:
*●27 tons 10 cwt
†‡§¶28 tons 5 cwt
Boiler pressure: 150 lb/sq in NS
Cylinders: (I) 12″×20″,
‡$14\frac{3}{16}$″×20″
Driving wheel diameter: 4′ 0″
Tractive effort: 7,650 lb,
‡10,695 lb
Valve gear: Stephenson (slide valves)

*82 (—) Boxhill[1]
‡72 (32636) Fenchurch[2]
†11 (32640) Newport[3]
§46 (32646) Newington[4]
†50 (32650) Sutton[5]
†55 (32655) Stepney[2]
†62 (32662) Martello[6]
¶3 (32670) Bodiam[7]
†78 (32678) Knowle[8]
●54 (DS680) Waddon[9]

Class Q1 0-6-0

Introduced 1942. Bulleid "Austerity" design with multiple-jet blastpipe and large diameter chimney.

Preserved by BRB. On loan to Bulleid Society at the Bluebell Railway, Sheffield Park.

Weight:
Locomotive: 51 tons 5 cwt
Tender: 38 tons
Boiler pressure: 230 lb/sq in Su
Cylinders: (I) 19"×26"
Driving wheel diameter: 5' 1"
Tractive effort: 30,080 lb
Valve gear: Stephenson (piston valves)

33001 (CI)

Class WC & BB 4-6-2
"West Country and Battle of Britain"

*__WC.__ Introduced 1945. Bulleid lightweight development of his Merchant Navy class with air-smoothed casing, high pressure boiler, multiple-jet blastpipe and chain-driven Bulleid valve gear. Boiler pressure subsequently reduced. Originally intended for use in West of England and given a "West Country" name.

†**BB.** Introduced 1946. Identical in all respects to WC class, but originally intended for use on Eastern Section and given "Battle of Britain" name.

‡Locomotives of both type, rebuilt from 1957 with Walschaerts valve gear, multiple-jet blastpipe and large diameter chimney. Air-smoothed casing removed.

[1] Preserved at the Mid-Hants Railway, New Alresford.

[2] Preserved by the Bulleid Society Ltd at the Bluebell Railway, Sheffield Park.

[3] Preserved by the Main Line Steam Trust, Loughborough Central.

[4] Preserved by BRB. On loan to Great Western Society, Didcot.

[5] Preserved by the Battle of Britain Locomotive Preservation Society at the Nene Valley Railway, Wansford.

[6] Preserved at the Keighley & Worth Valley Railway, Haworth.

Weight:
Locomotive: 86 tons
‡90 tons 1 cwt
Boiler pressure: 250 lb/sq in Su
Cylinders: Three, $16\frac{3}{8}$"×24"
Driving wheel diameter: 6' 2"
Tractive effort: 27,715 lb
Valve gear: Bulleid (piston valves)
‡Walschaerts (piston valves)

*‡34016 Bodmin[1]
*21C123 (34023) Blackmore Vale[2]
*‡34039 Boscastle[3]
†34051 Winston Churchill[4]
†34081 92 Squadron[5]
*34092 City of Wells[6]
*34105 Swanage[1]

Class MN 4-6-2
"Merchant Navy"

Introduced 1941. Bulleid design with air-smoothed casing, high pressure boiler, multiple-jet blastpipe and chain-driven Bulleid valve gear. Rebuilt from 1956 with lower boiler pressure, Walschaerts valve gear, multiple-jet blastpipe and large-diameter chimney. Air smoothed casing removed.

[1] Preserved at Steamtown, Carnforth.
[2] Preserved by Merchant Navy Locomotive Society at Hereford.
[3] Preserved as sectioned exhibit at the National Railway Museum, York.

Weight:
Locomotive: 97 tons 18 cwt
Boiler pressure: 250 lb/sq in Su
Cylinders: Three, 18" × 24"
Driving wheel diameter: 6' 2"
Tractive effort: 33, 495 lb
Valve gear: Walschaerts (piston valves)

35005 Canadian Pacific[1]
35028 Clan Line[2]
35029 Ellerman Lines[3]

Class O2 0-4-4T

Introduced 1889. Adams LSWR design. Transferred to Isle of Wight in 1925 and fitted with Westinghouse brake. Fitted with enlarged bunker in 1932.
Preserved by Wight Locomotive Society at Havenstreet.

Weight: 48 tons 8 cwt
Boiler pressure: 160 lb/sq in NS
Cylinders: (I) $17\frac{1}{2}$" × 24"
Driving wheel diameter: 4' 10"
Tractive effort: 17,235 lb
Valve gear: Stephenson (slide valves)

24 (W24) Calbourne

Ex-SR Class Q1 0-6-0 No. 33001 [J. Scrace

L.M.S. Steam Locomotives

Class 4P 4-4-0

Introduced 1902. Johnson Midland compound, rebuilt 1914 to Deeley design. Subsequently fitted with superheater.
Preserved at the National Railway Museum, York.

Weight:
Locomotive: 61 tons 14 cwt
Boiler pressure: 200 lb/sq in Su
Cylinders: Three:
(O) 21" × 26" (two, low pressure)
(I) 19" × 26" (one, high pressure)
Driving wheel diameter: 7' 0"
Tractive effort: 21,840 lb (of l.p. cylinders at 80 per cent boiler pressure)
Valve gear: Stephenson (l.p., slide valves; h.p., piston valves)

1000 (41000)

Class 2MT 2-6-2T

Introduced 1946. Ivatt design.
[1]Preserved at the Keighley & Worth Valley Railway, Haworth.
[2]Preserved by the Ivatt Trust at Quainton Road.
[3]Preserved by the Caerphilly Railway Society.

Weight: 63 tons 5 cwt
Boiler pressure: 200 lb/sq in Su
Cylinders:
(O) 16" × 24", *$16\frac{1}{2}$" × 24"
Driving wheel diameter: 5' 0"
Tractive effort: 17,410 lb, *18,510 lb
Valve gear: Walschaerts (piston valves)

41241[1] *41312[3]
*41298[2] *41313[2]

Class 1F 0-6-0T

Introduced 1878. Johnson Midland design. Rebuilt with Belpaire firebox. Preserved by the 1708 Locomotive Preservation Trust Ltd. At present in store at Dunstable.

Weight: 39 tons 11 cwt
Boiler pressure: 140 lb/sq in NS
Cylinders: (I) 17" × 24"
Driving wheel diameter: 4' 7"
Tractive effort: 15,005 lb
Valve gear: Stephenson (slide valves)

1708 (41708)

Class 3P 4-4-2T

Introduced 1909. Whitelegg LTSR "79" class.
Preserved by BRB. On loan to Bressingham Hall, Diss.

Weight: 71 tcns 10 cwt
Boiler pressure: 170 lb/sq in NS
Cylinders: (O) 19" × 26"
Driving wheel diameter: 6' 6"
Tractive effort: 17,390 lb
Valve gear: Stephenson (slide valves)

80 (41966) Thundersley

Class 4MT 2-6-4T

Introduced 1945. Fairburn development of Stanier design with shorter wheelbase and detail alterations.
Preserved by the Lakeside Railway, Haverthwaite.
[1]Painted in LNWR black livery
[2]Painted in CR blue livery

Weight: 85 tons 5 cwt
Boiler pressure: 200 lb/sq in Su
Cylinders: (O) $19\frac{5}{8}$" × 26"
Driving wheel diameter: 5' 9"
Tractive effort: 24, 670 lb
Valve gear: Walschaerts (piston valves)

2073 (42073)[1] 2085 (42085)[2]

Ex-LNWR 2-4-0 No. 790 Hardwicke [*G. W. Morrison*

Ex-MR Compound 4-4-0 No. 1000 [*Crown Copyright Reserved*

Class 4P 2-6-4T

Introduced 1934. Stanier three-cylinder design for LTS line.
Preserved by BRB. On loan to Bressingham Hall, Diss.
Weight: 92 tons 5 cwt
Boiler pressure: 200 lb/sq in Su
Cylinders: Three, 16″×26″
Driving wheel diameter: 5′ 9″
Tractive effort: 24,600 lb
Valve gear: Walschaerts (piston valves)

42500

Class 5MT 2-6-0

Introduced 1926. Hughes LMS design built under Fowler's direction.
[1]Preserved at the National Railway Museum, York.
Weight:
Locomotive: 66 tons
Boiler pressure: 180 lb/sq in Su
Cylinders: (O) 21″×26″
Driving wheel diameter: 5′ 6″
Tractive effort: 26,580 lb
Valve gear: Walschaerts (piston valves)

2700 (42700)[1]

Class 5MT 2-6-0

Introduced 1933. Stanier LMS design.
Preserved by the Stanier Mogul Fund at the Severn Valley Railway, Bridgnorth.
Weight:
Locomotive: 69 tons 2 cwt
Boiler pressure: 225 lb/sq in Su
Cylinders: (O) 18″×28″
Driving wheel diameter: 5′ 6″
Tractive effort: 26,290 lb
Valve gear: Walschaerts (piston valves)

42968

Class 4MT 2-6-0

Introduced 1947. Ivatt design.
Preserved by the Severn Valley Railway, Bridgnorth.
Weight:
Locomotive: 59 tons 2 cwt
Boiler pressure: 225 lb/sq in Su
Cylinders: (O) 17½″×26″
Driving wheel diameter: 5′ 3″
Tractive effort: 24,170 lb
Valve gear: Walschaerts (piston valves)

43106

Class 4F 0-6-0

Introduced 1911. Fowler Midland design.
*Introduced 1924. Post-Grouping development of Midland design, with reduced boiler mountings.
[1]Preserved at the Keighley & Worth Valley Railway, Haworth.
[2]Preserved by BRB, at Midland Railway Trust. Butterley.
[3]Preserved by the North Staffordshire Railway Society at Cheddleton.
Weight:
Locomotive: 48 tons 15 cwt
Boiler pressure: 175 lb/sq in Su
Cylinders: (I) 20″×26″
Driving wheel diameter: 5′ 3″
Tractive effort: 24,555 lb
Valve gear: Stephenson (piston valves)

43924[1] *44422[3]
*4027 (44027)[2]

Class 5MT 4-6-0

Introduced 1934. Stanier design.
*Introduced 1947. Outside Stephenson link motion and Timken roller bearings.
[1]Preserved at North Yorkshire Moors Railway, Grosmont.

[2]Preserved at Steamport Transport Museum, Southport.
[3]Preserved by Steamtown at Carnforth.
[4]Preserved by BRB; at present in store. To go to Severn Valley.
[5]Privately preserved at the Strathspey Railway, Boat of Garten.
[6]Preserved by the Stanier Black 5 Locomotive Preservation Society at Severn Valley Railway, Bridgnorth.
[7]Preserved at the Keighley & Worth Valley Railway, Haworth.
[8]Preserved by the Main Line Steam Trust at Loughborough Central.
[9]Preserved by Mr. A. E. Draper, restored by Humberside Locomotive Preservation Group and currently on loan to National Railway Museum, York.
[10]Preserved by the Bristol Suburban Railway Society, Bitton.
[11]Preserved by the Stanier Black 5 Preservation Society; at present on loan to the North Yorkshire Moors Railway, Grosmont.

Weight:
Locomotive: 72 tons 2 cwt
*75 tons 6 cwt
Boiler pressure: 225 lb/sq in Su
Cylinders: (O) 18½"×28"
Driving wheel diameter: 6' 0"
Tractive effort: 25,455 lb
Valve gear: Walschaerts (piston valves)
*Stephenson

*4767 (44767) George Stephenson[1]
44806 Magpie[2]
44871[3]
44932[3]
45000[4]
5025 (45025)[5]
45110 RAF Biggin Hill[6]
45212[7]
5231 (45231) 3rd (Volunteer) Battalion The Worcestershire and Sherwood Foresters Regiment[8]
45305[9]
45379[10]
5407 (45407)[3]
5428 (45428) Eric Treacy[11]

Class 6P5F 4-6-0 "Jubilee"

Introduced 1934. Stanier taper boiler development of the "Patriot" class.
*Fitted with double chimney in 1961.
[1]Preserved by 7029 Clun Castle Ltd at Tyseley.
[2]Preserved by the Bahamas Locomotive Society at Dinting Railway Centre.
[3]Preserved at Dinting Railway Centre.

Weight:
Locomotive: 79 tons 11 cwt
Boiler pressure: 225 lb/sq in Su
Cylinders: Three, 17"×26"
Driving wheel diameter: 6' 9"
Tractive effort: 26,610 lb
Valve gear: Walschaerts (piston valves)

5593 (45593) Kolhapur[1]
*5596 (45596) Bahamas[2]
5690 (45690) Leander[3]

Class 7P 4-6-0 "Royal Scot"

Introduced 1943. Stanier rebuild of Fowler locomotives (introduced 1927) with taper boiler, new cylinders and double chimney.
[1]Preserved at Bressingham Hall, Diss.
[2]Preserved at Dinting Railway Centre.

Weight:
Locomotive: 83 tons
Boiler pressure: 250 lb/sq in Su
Cylinders: Three, 18"×26"
Driving wheel diameter: 6' 9"
Tractive effort: 33,150 lb
Valve gear: Walschaerts (piston valves)

6100 (46100) Royal Scot[1]
6115 (46115) Scots Guardsman[2]

Class 7P 4-6-2 "Princess Royal"

Introduced 1933. Stanier design.
*Introduced 1935. Development of original design with modifications to valve gear, boiler and other details.
[1] Preserved by the Princess Elizabeth Locomotive Society at Hereford.
[2] Preserved at the Midland Railway Trust, Butterley.

Weight:
Locomotive: 104 tons 10 cwt
Boiler pressure: 250 lb/sq in Su
Cylinders: Four, $16\frac{1}{4}'' \times 28''$
Driving wheel diameter: 6′ 6″
Tractive effort: 40,285 lb
Valve gear: Walschaerts (piston valves)

6201 (46201) Princess Elizabeth[1]
*6203 (46203) Princess Margaret Rose[2]

Class 8P 4-6-2 "Coronation"

Introduced 1937. Stanier enlargement of "Princess Royal" Class.
*Originally streamlined, but casing removed 1946–1949.
[1] Preserved at The National Railway Museum, York (on loan from Butlins Ltd).
[2] Preserved at Bressingham Hall, Diss
[3] Preserved at the Birmingham Museum of Science & Industry.

Weight:
Locomotive: 105 tons 5 cwt
Boiler pressure: 250 lb/sq in Su
Cylinders: Four, $16\frac{1}{2}'' \times 28''$
Driving wheel diameter: 6′ 9″
Tractive effort: 40,000 lb
Valve gear: Walschaerts with rocking shafts (piston valves)

*46229 Duchess of Hamilton[1]
6233 (46233) Duchess of Sutherland[2]
*46235 City of Birmingham[3]

Class 2MT 2-6-0

Introduced 1946. Ivatt design.
[1] Preserved by Steamtown at Carnforth.
[2] Preserved by the Severn Valley Railway, Bridgnorth.
[3] Preserved by the Ivatt Trust at Quainton Road.
[4] Preserved by the 46464 Preservation Trust at the Strathspey Railway, Aviemore.
[5] Preserved by the Strathspey Railway; at present at the Severn Valley Railway, Bridgnorth.

Weight:
Locomotive: 47 tons 2 cwt
Boiler pressure: 200 lb/sq in Su
Cylinders:
(O) $16'' \times 24''$, (O) $16\frac{1}{2}'' \times 24''$
Driving wheel diameter: 5′ 0″
Tractive effort: 17,410 lb, *18,510 lb
Valve gear: Walschaerts (piston valves)

6441 (46441)[1]
46443[2]
46447[3]
46464[4]
*46512[5]
*46521[2]

Class 3F 0-6-0T

Introduced 1924. Post-Grouping development of Fowler Midland design with detail alterations.
[1] Preserved by the Liverpool Locomotive Preservation Group at Steamport Transport Museum, Southport.
[2] Preserved by the Midland Railway Trust, Butterley.
[3] Privately preserved at the Severn Valley Railway, Bridgnorth.
[4] Preserved at the East Somerset Railway, Cranmore.

Above: Ex-LMSR "Jubilee" Class 4-6-0 No. 5690 Leander
[*N. E. Preedy*

Right: Ex-LMSR Class 4MT 2-6-0 No. 43106
[*J. Scrace*

Below: Ex-LMSR Class 8F 2-8-0 No. 8233
[*Stanier 8F Society*

Weight: 49 tons 10 cwt
Boiler pressure: 160 lb/sq in NS
Cylinders: (I) 18"×26"
Driving wheel diameter: 4' 7"
Tractive effort: 20,835 lb
Valve gear: Stephenson (slide valves)

47298[1]
47327[2]
16440 (47357)[2]
47383[3]
47445[2]
47493[4]
47564[2]

Class 8F 2-8-0

Introduced 1935. Stanier design.
[1]Preserved by the Yorkshire Dales Railway Society at Embsay
[2]Preserved at the Keighley & Worth Valley Railway, Haworth.
[3]Preserved by the 8F Preservation Society at Bridgnorth.

Weight: ·
Locomotive: 72 tons 2 cwt
Boiler pressure: 225 lb/sq in Su
Cylinders: (O) $18\frac{1}{2}$"×28"
Driving wheel diameter: 4' $8\frac{1}{2}$"
Tractive effort: 32,440 lb
Valve gear: Walschaerts (piston valves)

48151[1]
8431 (48431)[2]
8233 (48773)[3]

Class 7F 0-8-0

Introduced 1921. Beames development of LNWR G2 class, with higher pressure boiler. Later rebuilt with Belpaire boiler.
Preserved at Ironbridge Gorge Museum, Telford, Shropshire.

Weight:
Locomotive: 62 tons
Boiler pressure: 175 lb/sq in Su
Cylinders: (I) $20\frac{1}{2}$"×24"
Driving wheel diameter: 4' $5\frac{1}{2}$"
Tractive effort: 28,045 lb
Valve gear: Joy (piston valves)

49395

Class 2P 2-4-2T

Introduced 1889. Aspinall LYR Class 5.
Preserved by BRB, at the National Railway Museum, York.

Weight: 55 tons 19 cwt
Boiler pressure: 180 lb/sq in NS
Cylinders: (I) 18"×26"
Driving wheel diameter: 5' 8"
Tractive effort: 18,955 lb
Valve gear: Joy (slide valves)

1008 (50621)

Class 0F 0-4-0ST

Introduced 1891. Aspinall LYR Class 21.
*Sold by the LMS.
Preserved at the Keighley & Worth Valley Railway, Haworth.

Weight: 21 tons 5 cwt
Boiler pressure: 160 lb/sq in NS
Cylinders: (O) 13"×18"
Driving wheel diameter: 3' $0\frac{3}{8}$"
Tractive effort: 11,335 lb
Valve gear: Stephenson (slide valves)

51218
*19(11243)

Class 2F 0-6-0

Introduced 1887. Barton-Wright LYR Class 25.
Preserved at the Keighley & Worth Valley Railway, Haworth.

Weight:
Locomotive: 39 tons 1 cwt
Boiler pressure: 140 lb/sq in NS
Cylinders: (I) $17\frac{1}{2}$"×26"
Driving wheel diameter: 4' 6"
Tractive effort: 17,545 lb
Valve gear: Stephenson (slide valves)

957 (52044)

Class 3F 0-6-0

Introduced 1889. Aspinall LYR Class 27.
Privately preserved at Steamtown, Carnforth.

Weight:
Locomotive: 42 tons 3 cwt
Boiler pressure: 180 lb/sq in NS
Cylinders: (I) 18" × 26"
Driving wheel diameter: 5' 1"
Tractive effort: 21,130 lb
Valve gear: Joy (slide valves)

1122 (52322)

Class 7F 2-8-0

Introduced 1925. Large-boiler development of Fowler SDJR design (introduced 1914). Rebuilt with smaller boiler by BR.
[1] Preserved by the Somerset & Dorset Railway Museum Trust at the West Somerset Railway.
[2] To be preserved at the North Yorkshire Moors Railway.

Weight:
Locomotive: 64 tons 15 cwt
Boiler pressure: 190 lb/sq in Su
Cylinders: (O) 21" × 28"
Driving wheel diameter: 4' 8½"
Tractive effort: 35,295 lb
Valve gear: Walschaerts (piston valves)

53808[1]
53809[2]

Class 2P 0-4-4T

Introduced 1900. McIntosh Caledonian "439" or "Standard Passenger" class.
Preserved by the Scottish Railway Preservation Society, Falkirk.

Weight: 53 tons 19 cwt
Boiler pressure: 180 lb/sq in NS
Cylinders: (I) 18" × 26"
Driving wheel diameter: 5' 9"
Tractive effort: 18,680 lb
Valve gear: Stephenson (slide valves)

419 (55189)

Class 3F 0-6-0

Introduced 1899. McIntosh Caledonian "812" class.
Preserved at Glasgow Transport Museum.

Weight:
Locomotive: 45 tons 14 cwt
Boiler pressure: 180 lb/sq in NS
Cylinders: (I) 18½" × 26"
Driving wheel diameter: 5' 0"
Tractive effort: 22,690 lb
Valve gear: Stephenson (slide valves)

828 (57566)

Class 2F 0-6-0T

Introduced 1879. Park NLR design.
Preserved by Bluebell Railway at Sheffield Park.

Weight: 45 tons 10 cwt
Boiler pressure: 160 lb/sq in NS
Cylinders: (O) 17" × 24"
Driving wheel diameter: 4' 4"
Tractive effort: 18,140 lb
Valve gear: Stephenson (slide valves)

2650 (58850)

Class 2F 0-6-2T

Introduced 1882. Webb LNWR "Coal Tank".
Preserved by the National Trust at Dinting Railway Centre.

Weight: 43 tons 15 cwt
Boiler pressure: 150 lb/sq in NS
Cylinders: (I) 17" × 24"
Driving wheel diameter: 4' 5½"
Tractive effort: 16,530 lb
Valve gear: Stephenson (slide valves)

1054 (58926)

"Jones Goods" 4-6-0

Introduced 1894, Jones Highland Goods design. Withdrawn 1934 as LMS No. 17916 for preservation. Restored to original condition and returned to service for special use 1959–61.

Preserved at Glasgow Transport Museum.

Weight:
Locomotive: 56 tons
Boiler pressure: 175 lb/sq in NS
Cylinders: (O) 20″ × 26″
Driving wheel diameter: 5′ 3″
Tractive effort: 24,555 lb
Valve gear: Stephenson (slide valves)

103

"Caledonian Single" 4-2-2

Introduced 1886. Neilson & Co. design for the Caledonian Railway incorporating Drummond details. Withdrawn as LMS No. 14010 in 1935. Restored to Caledonian livery and returned to service for special use 1958–61.

Preserved at Glasgow Transport Museum.

Weight:
Locomotive and Tender: 75 tons
Boiler pressure: 150 lb/sq in NS
Cylinders: (I) 18″ × 26″
Driving wheel diameter: 7′ 0″
Tractive effort: 12,785 lb
Valve gear: Stephenson (slide valves)

123

L.N.E.R. Steam Locomotives

Class A4 4-6-2

Introduced 1935. Gresley streamlined design. All fitted with double chimney.
*Fitted with corridor tender.
[1]Preserved by the A4 Locomotive Society.
[2]Preserved at Green Bay, Wisconsin, USA.
[3]Privately preserved at Markinch, Fife.
[4]Preserved at Montreal Railway Historical Museum, Canada.
[5]Privately preserved at Walton Colliery.
[6]Preserved at the National Railway Museum, York.

Weight:
Locomotive: 102 tons 19 cwt
Tender: *64 tons 19 cwt
60 tons 7 cwt
Boiler pressure: 250 lb/sq in Su
Cylinders:
Three, 18½" × 26"
Driving wheel diameter: 6' 8"
Tractive effort: 35,455 lb
Valve gear: Walschaerts, with derived motion (piston valves)

*4498 (60007) Sir Nigel Gresley[1]
60008 Dwight D. Eisenhower[2]
*60009 Union of South Africa[3]
*60010 Dominion of Canada[4]
19 (60019) Bittern[5]
4468 (60022) Mallard[6]

Class A3 4-6-2

Introduced 1922. Gresley GNR design, later rebuilt with higher pressure boiler. Fitted with double chimney in 1959.
Privately preserved with single chimney, corridor tender and water-carrying corridor tender at Steamtown, Carnforth.

Weight:
Locomotive: 96 tons 5 cwt
Tender: 64 tons 19 cwt
Boiler pressure: 220 lb/sq in Su
Cylinders: Three, 19" × 26"
Driving wheel diameter: 6' 8"
Tractive effort: 32,910 lb
Valve gear: Walschaerts, with derived motion (piston valves)

4472 (60103) Flying Scotsman

Class A2 4-6-2

Introduced 1947. Peppercorn development of Thompson Class A2/2 with shorter wheelbase. Later rebuilt with double chimney and multiple-valve regulator.
Preserved by the Blue Peter Society at Walton Colliery.

Weight:
Locomotive: 101 tons
Tender: 60 tons 7 cwt
Boiler pressure: 250 lb/sq in Su
Cylinders: Three, 19" × 26"
Driving wheel diameter: 6' 2"
Tractive effort: 40,430 lb
Valve gear: Walschaerts (piston valves)

532 (60532) Blue Peter

Class V2 2-6-2

Introduced 1936. Gresley design.
Preserved at the National Railway Museum, York.

Weight:
Locomotive: 93 tons 2 cwt
Tender: 52 tons
Boiler pressure: 220 lb/sq in Su
Cylinders: Three, 18½" × 26"
Driving wheel diameter: 6' 2"
Tractive effort: 33,730 lb
Valve gear: Walschaerts with derived motion (piston valves)

4771 (60800) Green Arrow

Class B1 4-6-0

Introduced 1942. Thompson design.
[1]Preserved by the Thompson B1 Locomotive Society at the Main Line Steam Trust, Loughborough.
[2]Preserved by the B1 Preservation Society at Steamtown, Carnforth.

Weight:
Locomotive: 71 tons 3 cwt
Tender: 52 tons
Boiler pressure: 225 lb/sq in Su
Cylinders: (O) 20"×26"
Driving wheel diameter: 6' 2"
Tractive effort: 26,880 lb
Valve gear: Walschaerts (piston valves)

1264 (61264)[1]
1306 (61306) Mayflower[2]

Class B12 4-6-0

B12/3 Introduced 1932. Gresley rebuild of Holden B12/1 (introduced 1911) with large round-topped boiler.
Preserved by the Midland & Great Northern Preservation Society, Sheringham.

Weight:
Locomotive: 69 tons 10 cwt
Tender: 39 tons 6 cwt
Boiler pressure: 180 lb/sq in Su
Cylinders: (I) 20"×28"
Driving wheel diameter: 6' 6"
Tractive effort: 21,970 lb
Valve gear: Stephenson (piston valves)

61572

Class K4 2-6-0

Introduced 1937. Gresley design.
Preserved at the Severn Valley Railway, Bridgnorth.

Weight:
Locomotive: 68 tons 8 cwt
Tender: 44 tons 4 cwt
Boiler pressure: 200 lb/sq in Su
Cylinders: Three, $18\frac{1}{2}$"×26"
Driving wheel diameter: 5' 2"
Tractive effort: 36,600 lb
Valve gear: Walschaerts, with derived motion (piston valves)

3442 (61994) The Great Marquess

Class K1 2-6-0

Introduced 1949. Peppercorn development of Thompson K1/1 (rebuilt from Gresley K4) with increased length.
Preserved by the North Eastern Locomotive Preservation Group at the North Yorkshire Moors Railway, Grosmont.

Weight:
Locomotive: 66 tons 17 cwt
Tender: 44 tons 4 cwt
Boiler pressure: 225 lb/sq in Su
Cylinders: (O) 20"×26"
Driving wheel diameter: 5' 2"
Tractive effort: 32,080 lb
Valve gear: Walschaerts (piston valves)

2005 (62005)

Class D40 4-4-0

Introduced 1920. Heywood GNSR superheated development of Pickersgill 1899 design. Restored to original condition and returned to service for special use 1959–61.
Preserved at Glasgow Transport Museum.

Weight:
Locomotive: 48 tons 13 cwt
Tender: 37 tons 8 cwt
Boiler pressure: 165 lb/sq in Su
Cylinders: (I) 18"×26"
Driving wheel diameter: 6' 1"
Tractive effort: 16,185 lb
Valve gear: Stephenson (slide valves)

49 (62277) Gordon Highlander

Class D34 4-4-0

Introduced 1913. Reid NBR design. Restored to NBR livery and returned to service for special use. 1959–61. Preserved at Glasgow Transport Museum.

Weight:
Locomotive: 57 tons 4 cwt
Tender: 46 tons 13 cwt
Boiler pressure: 165 lb/sq in Su
Cylinders: (I) 20″×26″
Driving wheel diameter: 6′ 0″
Tractive effort: 20,260 lb
Valve gear: Stephenson (piston valves)

256 (62469) Glen Douglas

Class D11 4-4-0

D11/1 Introduced 1920. Robinson GCR "Large Director" development of D10.
Preserved by the BRB; on loan to the Main Line Steam Trust, Loughborough.

Weight:
Locomotive: 61 tons 3 cwt
Tender: 48 tons 6 cwt
Boiler pressure: 180 lb/sq in Su
Cylinders: (I) 20″×26″
Driving wheel diameter: 6′ 9″
Tractive effort: 19,645 lb
Valve gear: Stephenson (piston valves)

506 (62660) Butler-Henderson

Class D49 4-4-0

D49/1 Introduced 1927. Gresley design.
Preserved by the Royal Scottish Museum, Edinburgh; on loan to the Scottish Railway Preservation Society, Falkirk.

Weight:
Locomotive: 66 tons
Tender: 48 tons 6 cwt
Boiler pressure: 180 lb/sq in Su
Cylinders: Three, 17″×26″
Driving wheel diameter: 6′ 8″
Tractive effort: 21,555 lb
Valve gear: Walschaerts, with derived motion (piston valves)

246 (62712) Morayshire

Class E4 2-4-0

Introduced 1891. J. Holden GER design.
Preserved at the National Railway Museum, York.

Weight:
Locomotive: 40 tons 6 cwt
Tender: 30 tons 13 cwt
Boiler pressure: 160 lb/sq in NS
Cylinders: (I) 17½″×24″
Driving wheel diameter: 5′ 8″
Tractive effort: 14,700 lb
Valve gear: Stephenson (slide valves)

490 (62785)

Class Q6 0-8-0

Introduced 1913. Raven NER design. Preserved by the North Eastern Locomotive Preservation Group at the North Yorkshire Moors Railway, Grosmont.

Weight:
Locomotive: 65 tons 18 cwt
Tender: 44 tons 2 cwt
Boiler pressure: 180 lb/sq in Su
Cylinders: (O) 20″×26″
Driving wheel diameter: 4′ 7¼″
Tractive effort: 28,800 lb
Valve gear: Stephenson (piston valves)

3395 (63395)

Class Q7 0-8-0

Introduced 1919. Raven NER design. Scheduled for preservation by BRB; at present in store at Preston Park pending restoration.

Scheduled for preservation by BRB. At National Railway Museum, York (not on display).

Weight:
Locomotive: 71 tons 12 cwt
Tender: 44 tons 2 cwt
Boiler pressure: 180 lb/sq in Su
Cylinders: Three, $18\frac{1}{2}'' \times 26''$
Driving wheel diameter: 4′ $7\frac{1}{4}''$
Tractive effort: 36,965 lb
Valve gear: Stephenson (piston valves)

63460

Class O4 2-8-0

O4/1 Introduced 1911. Robinson GCR design.
Preserved by BRB. On loan to Dinting Railway Centre.

Weight:
Locomotive: 73 tons 4 cwt
Tender: 48 tons 6 cwt
Boiler pressure: 180 lb/sq in Su
Cylinders: (O) $21'' \times 26''$
Driving wheel diameter: 4′ 8″
Tractive effort: 31,325 lb
Valve gear: Stephenson (piston valves)

102 (63601)

Class J21 0-6-0

Introduced 1886. T. W. Worsdell NER design.
Preserved at the North of England open Air Museum, Beamish.

Weight:
Locomotive: 43 tons 15 cwt
Tender: 36 tons 19 cwt
Boiler pressure: 160 lb/sq in Su
Cylinders: (I) $19'' \times 24''$
Driving wheel diameter: 5′ $1\frac{1}{4}''$
Tractive effort: 19,240 lb
Valve gear: Stephenson (piston valves)

876 (65033)

Class J36 0-6-0

Introduced 1888. Holmes NBR design.
Preserved by the Scottish Railway Preservation Society, Falkirk.

Weight:
Locomotive: 41 tons 19 cwt
Tender: 33 tons 9 cwt
Boiler pressure: 165 lb/sq in NS
Cylinders: (I) $18\frac{1}{4}'' \times 26''$
Driving wheel diameter: 5′ 0″
Tractive effort: 19,690 lb
Valve gear: Stephenson (slide valves)

673 (65243) Maude

Class J15 0-6-0

Introduced 1883. T. W. Worsdell GER design.
Preserved by the Midland & Great Northern Preservation Society, Sheringham.

Weight:
Locomotive: 37 tons 2 cwt
Tender: 30 tons 13 cwt
Boiler pressure: 160 lb/sq in NS
Cylinders: (I) $17\frac{1}{2}'' \times 24''$
Driving wheel diameter: 4′ 11″
Tractive effort: 16,940 lb
Valve gear: Stephenson (slide valves)

564 (65462)

Class J17 0-6-0

Introduced 1902. J. Holden GER design.
Preserved by BRB; at present on loan to Bressingham Hall, Diss.

Weight:
Locomotive: 45 tons 8 cwt
Tender: 38 tons 5 cwt

Ex-LNER Class K1 2-6-0 No. 2005 [*I. S. Carr*

EX-LNER Class A4 4-6-2 No. 4498 Sir Nigel Gresley [*P. J. Skelton*

Boiler pressure: 180 lb/sq in Su
Cylinders: (I) 19″ × 26″
Driving wheel diameter: 4′ 11″
Tractive effort: 24,340 lb
Valve gear: Stephenson (slide valves)

1217E (65567)

Class J27 0-6-0

Introduced 1921. Raven NER superheated development of W. Worsdell design (introduced 1906) with superheater and piston valves. Superheater later removed.
Preserved by the North Eastern Locomotive Preservation Group. On loan to York Museum.

Weight:
Locomotive: 47 tons
Tender: 36 tons 19 cwt
Boiler pressure: 180 lb/sq in NS
Cylinders: (I) $18\frac{1}{2}$″ × 26″
Driving wheel diameter: 4′ $7\frac{1}{4}$″
Tractive effort: 24,640 lb
Valve gear: Stephenson (piston valves)

2392 (65894)

Class J94 0-6-0ST

Introduced 1943. Riddles Ministry of Supply design, purchased by LNER, 1946.
Preserved at the Keighley & Worth Valley Railway, Haworth.

Weight: 48 tons 5 cwt
Boiler pressure: 170 lb/sq in NS
Cylinders: (I) 18″ × 26″
Driving wheel diameter: 4′ 3″
Tractive effort: 24,870 lb
Valve gear: Stephenson (slide valves)

68077

Class Y7 0-4-0T

Introduced 1888. T. W. Worsdell NER design.
*Sold by LNER.
[1]Preserved by the Y7 Preservation Society at the Main Line Steam Trust, Loughborough.
[2]Preserved by the Middleton Railway Trust, Hunslet, Leeds.

Weight: 22 tons 14 cwt
Boiler pressure: 140 lb/sq in NS
Cylinders: (I) 14″ × 20″
Driving wheel diameter: 3′ $6\frac{1}{4}$″
Tractive effort: 11,040 lb
Valve gear: Stephenson (slide valves)

68088[1] *1310[2]

Class Y9 0-4-0ST

Introduced 1882. Neilson & Co. design for NBR.
Preserved at Lytham Motive Power Museum, Helical Springs Ltd., Lytham St. Annes.

Weight: 27 tons 16 cwt
Boiler pressure: 130 lb/2q in NS
Cylinders: (O) 14″ × 20″
Driving wheel diameter: 3′ 8″
Tractive effort: 9,845 lb
Valve gear: Stephenson (slide valves)

42 (68095)

Class Y1 0-4-0T

Y1/2 Introduced 1927. Single-speed geared Sentinel Wagon Works design.
Preserved by the Middleton Railway Trust, Hunslet.

Weight: 19 tons 16 cwt
Boiler pressure: 275 lb/sq in Su

Above: Ex-NER Class T2 0-8-0 No. 2238
[*J. Hunt*

Right: Ex-GNR 4-4-2 No. 990 Henry Oakley
[*G. W. Morrison*

Below: Ex-LNER Class V2 2-6-2 No. 4771 Green Arrow
[*P. J. Skelton*

Cylinders: (I) $6\frac{3}{4}'' \times 9''$
Driving wheel diameter: 2′ 6″
Sprocket gear ratio: 11:25
Tractive effort: 7,260 lb
Valve gear: Sentinel (poppet valves)

59 (54, 68153)

Class J69 0-6-0T

Introduced 1902. J. Holden GER development of J67 (introduced 1890) with higher boiler pressure.
Preserved at the National Railway Museum, York.

Weight: 40 tons 9 cwt
Boiler pressure: 180 lb/sq in NS
Cylinders: (I) $16\frac{1}{2}'' \times 22''$
Driving wheel diameter: 4′ 0″
Tractive effort: 19,090 lb
Valve gear: Stephenson (slide valves)

87 (68633)

Class J52 0-6-0ST

J52/2 Introduced 1897. Ivatt GNR design.
Preserved by Captain W. G. Smith; at present on loan to the North Yorkshire Moors Railway, Grosmont.

Weight: 51 tons 14 cwt
Boiler pressure: 170 lb/sq in NS
Cylinders: (I) 18″ × 26″
Driving wheel diameter: 4′ 8″
Tractive effort: 21,735 lb
Valve gear: Stephenson (slide valves)

1247 (68846)

Class J72 0-6-0T

Introduced 1949. Development of W. Worsdell NER 1898 design. Now works enthusiasts' specials on the Derwent Valley Light Railway, York.

Weight: 38 tons 12 cwt
Boiler pressure: 140 lb/sq in NS
Cylinders: (I) 17″ × 24″
Driving wheel diameter: $4' \, 1\frac{1}{4}''$
Tractive effort: 16,760 lb
Valve gear: Stephenson (slide valves)

69023 Joem

Class N2 0-6-2T

N2/2 Introduced 1920. Gresley GNR design. Fitted with condensing apparatus and small chimney for working over Metropolitan line to Moorgate.
Preserved at the Main Line Steam Trust, Loughborough.

Weight: 70 tons 5 cwt
Boiler pressure: 170 lb/sq in Su
Cylinders: (I) 19″ × 26″
Driving wheel diameter: 5′ 8″
Tractive effort: 19,945 lb
Valve gear: Stephenson (piston valves)

4744 (69523)

Class N7 0-6 2T

N7/4 Introduced 1940. Rebuild of Hill GER design (introduced 1914) with round-topped boiler.
Preserved at the Stour Valley Railway, Chappel & Wakes Colne.

Weight: 61 tons 16 cwt
Boiler pressure: 180 lb/sq in Su
Cylinders: (I) 18″ × 24″
Driving wheel diameter: 4′ 10″
Tractive effort: 20,515 lb
Valve gear: Walschaerts (piston valves)

999E (69621)

B.R. Standard Locomotives

Class 7P6F 4-6-2

Introduced 1951. Designed at Derby.
[1]Preserved by the Britannia Locomotive Company at the Severn Valley Railway, Bridgnorth.
[2]Preserved by BRB. On loan to Bressingham Hall, Diss.

Weight:
Locomotive: 94 tons 4 cwt
Tender: 49 tons 3 cwt
Boiler pressure: 250 lb/sq in Su
Cylinders: (O) 20″×28″
Driving wheel diameter: 6′ 2″
Tractive effort: 32,150 lb
Valve gear: Walschaerts (piston valves)

70000 Britannia[1]
70013 Oliver Cromwell[2]

Class 8P 4-6-2

Introduced 1954. Designed at Derby. Preserved by 71000 Steam Locomotive Ltd at the Main Line Steam Trust, Loughborough.

Weight:
Locomotive: 101 tons 5 cwt
Tender: 53 tons 14 cwt
Boiler pressure: 250 lb/sq in Su
Cylinders: Three, 18″×28″
Driving wheel diameter: 6′ 2″
Tractive effort: 39,080 lb
Valve gear: Caprotti (poppet valves)

71000 Duke of Gloucester

Class 5MT 4-6-0

Introduced 1951. Designed at Doncaster.
[1]Preserved by the Peterborough Railway Society at the Nene Valley Railway, Wansford.
[2]Preserved by the Midland Railway Trust Ltd, Butterley.

Weight:
Locomotive: 76 tons 4 cwt
Tender: 52 tons 10 cwt
Boiler pressure: 225 lb/sq in Su
Cylinders: (O) 19″×28″
Driving wheel diameter: 6′ 2″
Tractive effort: 26,120 lb
Valve gear: Walschaerts (piston valves)
*Caprotti (poppet valves)

73050 City of Peterborough[1]
*73129[2]

Class 4MT 4-6-0

Introduced 1951. Designed at Brighton.
*Introduced 1957. Fitted with double chimney.
[1]Privately preserved at the Bluebell Railway, Sheffield Park.
[2]Preserved by the Shepherd Locomotive Trust at the East Somerset Railway, Cranmore.
[3]Preserved by the Severn Valley Railway, Bridgnorth.
[4]Preserved by the Standard 4 Locomotive Preservation Society at the Keighley & Worth Valley Railway, Haworth.

Weight:
Locomotive: 69 tons
Tender: 42 tons 3 cwt
Boiler pressure: 225 lb/sq in Su
Cylinders: (O) 18″×28″
Driving wheel diameter: 5′ 8″
Tractive effort: 25,100 lb
Valve gear: Walschaerts (piston valves)

75027[1]
*75029 The Green Knight[2]
*75069[3]
*75078[4]

Class 4MT 2-6-0

Introduced 1953. Designed at Doncaster.
[1]Preserved at Quainton Road.
[2]Preserved by Frogstone Ltd at Steamport Transport Museum, Southport.

Weight:
Locomotive: 59 tons 2 cwt
Boiler pressure: 225 lb/sq in Su
Cylinders: (O) $17\frac{1}{2}'' \times 26''$
Driving wheel diameter: 5′ 3″
Tractive effort: 24,170 lb
Valve gear: Walschaerts (piston valves)

76017[1] 76079[2]

Class 2MT 2-6-0

Introduced 1953. Designed at Derby.
[1]Preserved by the Severn Valley Railway, Bridgnorth.
[2]Preserved by the Standard Locomotive Preservation Society at the Keighley & Worth Valley Railway, Haworth.

Weight:
Locomotive: 49 tons 5 cwt
Boiler pressure: 200 lb/sq in
Cylinders: (O) $16\frac{1}{2}'' \times 24''$
Driving wheel diameter: 5′ 0″
Tractive effort: 18,515 lb
Valve gear: Walschaerts (piston valves)

78019[1] 78022[2]

Class 4MT 2-6-4T

Introduced 1951. Designed at Brighton.
[1]Preserved at the Keighley & Worth Valley Railway, Haworth.
[2]Preserved at the Dart Valley Railway, Buckfastleigh.
[3]Preserved by the Southern Steam Trust at Swanage.
[4]Preserved by the Severn Valley Railway, Bridgnorth.
[5]Preserved by the Locomotive Owners Group (Scotland) Ltd at Falkirk.
[6]Preserved at the North Yorkshire Moors Railway, Grosmont.
[7]Preserved by the Stour Valley Railway Preservation Society, Chappel & Wakes Colne.

Weight: 88 tons 10 cwt
Boiler pressure: 225 lb/sq in Su
Cylinders: (O) $18'' \times 28''$
Driving wheel diameter: 5′ 8″
Tractive effort: 25,100 lb
Valve gear: Walschaerts (piston valves)

80002[1] 80079[4] 80135[6]
80064[2] 80105[5] 80151[7]
80078[3]

Class 9F 2-10-0

Introduced 1954. Designed at Brighton. Fitted with double chimney.
[1]Preserved by the Shepherd locomotive Trust at the East Somerset Railway, Cranmore.
[2]Preserved at the National Railway Museum, York.

Weight:
Locomotive: 86 tons 14 cwt
Tender: 52 tons 10 cwt
Boiler pressure: 250 lb/sq in Su
Cylinders: (O) $20'' \times 28''$
Driving wheel diameter: 5′ 0″
Tractive effort: 39,670 lb
Valve gear: Walschaerts (piston valves)

92203 Black Prince[1]
92220 Evening Star[2]

Ex-BR Standard Class 4MT 2-6-4T No. 80079 [*N. E. Preedy*

Ex-BR Standard Class 9F 2-10-0 No. 92220 Evening Star [*P. J. Skelton*

Diesel Locomotives

Class 02
Yorkshire Engine Co. 0-4-0 Shunter

Introduced 1960. Yorkshire Engine Co. diesel-hydraulic shunting locomotive.

To be preserved by BRB in York Museum.

Engine:
Rolls-Royce C6NFL of 179 h.p. at 1,800 r.p.m.

Weight: 28 tons

Maximum tractive effort:
15,000 lb

Transmission:
Hydraulic. Rolls-Royce 3-stage torque converter, Series 10,000. Axle-hung double-reduction final drive with reversing mechanism

Driving wheel diameter: 3′ 6″

D2860

Class 03
British Railways 0-6-0 Shunter

Introduced 1957. Standard BR 204 b.h.p. diesel-mechanical shunting locomotive.

[1]Preserved at the National Railway Museum, York.

[2]Preserved by the Lakeside Railway, Haverthwaite.

[3]Preserved by the Dart Valley Railway, Buckfastleigh.

[4]Privately preserved at Steamtown, Carnforth.

Engine:
Gardner 8L3 of 204 b.h.p. at 1,200 r.p.m.

Weight: 30 tons

Maximum tractive effort:
15,650 lb

Transmission:
Mechanical. Vulcan-Sinclair type 23 fluid coupling. Wilson-Drewry C.A.5 type five-speed epicyclic gearbox. Type RF II spiral bevel reverse and final drive unit.

Driving wheel diameter: 3′ 7″

03 090[1]	D2192[3]
8 (D2117)[2]	D2381[4]

Class 04
Drewry 0-6-0 Shunter

Introduced 1952 (*1955). Drewry 204 b.h.p. diesel-mechanical shunting locomotive.

[1]Preserved by the North Yorkshire Moors Railway, Grosmont.

[2]Preserved by the Midland Railway Trust Ltd, Butterley.

Engine:
Gardner 8L3 of 204 b.h.p. at 1,200 r.p.m.

Weight: 30 tons (*32 tons)

Maximum tractive effort:
16,850 lb (*15,650 lb)

Transmission:
Mechanical. Vulcan-Sinclair type 23 fluid coupling. Wilson-Drewry C.A.5 type five-speed epicyclic gearbox. Type RF II spiral bevel reverse and final drive unit

Driving wheel diameter:
3′ 3″ (*3′ 6″)

2207[1]   *2271[2]

Class 24/0
British Railways Bo-Bo Type 2

Introduced 1958. Standard Sulzer-engined Type 2 locomotive built by British Railways workshops.

Preserved at the North Yorkshire Moors Railway, Grosmont.

Engine:
Sulzer 6-cyl. 6LDA28 of 1,160 b.h.p. at 750 r.p.m.
Weight: 80 tons
Brake force: 38 tons
Maximum tractive effort:
40,000 lb
Transmission:
Electric. Four B.T.H. axle-hung nose-suspended traction motors of 213 h.p. (continuous rating)
Driving wheel diameter: 3′ 9″
Route availability: 6
Maximum speed: 75 m.p.h.

D5032 (24 032)

Class 31/0
British Railways AIA-AIA
Type 2

Introduced 1957.

Preserved in the National Railway Museum, York.

Engine:
English Electric 12-cyl. 12SV of 1,470 b.h.p.
Weight: 109 tons
Brake force: 49 tons
Maximum tractive effort:
42,000 lb
Transmission:
Electric. Four Brush traction motors, single reduction gear drive
Driving wheel diameter: 3′ 7″
Route availability: 5
Maximum speed: 80 m.p.h.
Fitted with electro-magnetic control equipment
D5500 (31018)

Class 35
Beyer Peacock (Hymek) B-B
Type 3

Introduced 1961. Medium-power diesel-hydraulic type for the Western Region.
[1] Preserved by the Diesel and Electric Group at the West Somerset Railway.
[2] Privately preserved at Didcot.
[3] Privately preserved at Swindon.

Engine:
Bristol-Siddeley/Maybach MD870 of 1,700 b.h.p.
Weight: 75 tons
Brake force: 33 tons
Maximum tractive effort:
49,700 lb
Transmission:
Hydraulic. Stone-Maybach Mekydro type 6184U
Driving wheel diameter: 3′ 9″
Route availability: 6
Maximum speed: 90 m.p.h.

7017[1] 7018[2] 7029[3]

Class 42
British Railways "Warship" B-B
Type 4

Introduced 1958. Swindon-built version of the "Warship", with four-wheeled bogies and Maybach engines.
Privately preserved at Swindon.

Engines:
Two Bristol Siddeley-Maybach MD 650 V-type of 1,152 b.h.p. at 1,530 r.p.m.
Weight: 78 tons
Maximum tractive effort:
52,400 lb
Transmission:
Hydraulic. Two Mekydro type K104 hydraulic transmissions containing permanently filled single torque converter and four-speed automatic gearbox
Driving wheel diameter: 3′ 3½″

821 Greyhound

Class 52 British Railways C-C Type 4

Introduced 1961.

[1] Privately preserved at Merehead. To be renamed Western Yeoman.
[2] Preserved by the Western Locomotive Association on the Dart Valley Railway (Torbay Line).
[3] Preserved on the Dart Valley Railway (Torbay Line).
[4] To be preserved at the National Railway Museum, York.

Engines:
Two Maybach MD655 12-cyl. V-type of 1,350 b.h.p. at 1,500 r.p.m.
Weight: 109 tons
Brake force: 50 tons
Maximum tractive effort: 72,600 lb.

Transmission:
Hydraulic. Two Voith-North British L630rV hydraulic transmissions, each containing three torque converters
Driving wheel diameter: 3′ 7″
Route availability: 6
Maximum speed: 90 m.p.h.
All dual braked

1010 Western Campaigner[1]
1013 Western Ranger[3]
1023 Western Fusilier[4]
1062 Western Courier[2]

English Electric Co-Co Type 5

Introduced 1955. Experimental high horse power locomotive. Ran trials on West Coast and East Coast expresses until 1960.
Preserved at the Science Museum, London.

Engines:
Two 18-cyl. Napier "Deltic" 18-25 of 1,650 b.h.p. at 1,500 r.p.m.
Weight: 106 tons
Maximum tractive effort:
60,000 lb
Transmission:
Electric. Six English Electric EE750 25G axle-hung nose-suspended traction motors
Driving wheel diameter: 3′ 7″

Deltic

English Electric 0-6-0 Shunter

Introduced 1957. One of two similar locomotives used for comparative trials between electric and hydraulic transmission.
Preserved at the Keighley & Worth Valley Railway, Haworth.

Engine:
English Electric 6RKT of 500 b.h.p. at 750 r.p.m.

Weight: 48 tons
Maximum tractive effort:
33,000 lb
Transmission:
Electric. One English Electric traction motor coupled to double-reduction gear-box final drive
Driving wheel diameter: 4′ 0″

D0226

Preserved Class 35 B-B No. D7018

Preserved Ex-GWR diesel railcar No. W20W [*J. Scrace*

Preserved Class 52 C-C No. D1062 Western Courier [*M. S. Wilkins*

Multiple Units

Class 100 (2) ■
Gloucester R. C. & W. Co.
Motor brake Second

Introduced 1957.
Preserved by the North Yorkshire Moors Railway, Grosmont.

Engines:
Two B.U.T. (A.E.C.) 6-cyl. horizontal type of 150 b.h.p.
Body: 57′ 6″ × 9′ 3″
Weight: 30 tons 5 cwt
Seats: 2nd, 52
Transmission:
Mechanical. Standard

SC50341 E51118

Class 103 (2) ■
Park Royal Vehicles
Motor Brake Second

Introduced 1957.
Preserved by the West Somerset Railway.

Engines:
Two B.U.T. (A.E.C.) 6-cyl. horizontal type of 150 b.h.p.
Body: 57′ 6″ × 9′ 3″
Weight: 33 tons 8 cwt
Seats: 2nd, 52
Transmission:
Mechanical. Standard

W50413 W50414

Class 143 (2) ■
Gloucester R. C. & W. Co.
Driving Trailer Composite (L)

Introduced 1957.
[1]Preserved by the North Yorkshire Moors Railway, Grosmont.
[2]Preserved by the Chacewater Light Railway Co.
[3]Preserved by the Gwili Railway Company Ltd.

Body: 57′ 6″ × 9′ 3″
Seats: 1st, 12; **2nd,** 54
Weight: 25 tons

SC56097[1] E56301[2] E56317[3] E56099[1]

Park Royal Vehicles (2) ■
Driving Trailer Composite (L)

Introduced 1957
Preserved by the West Somerset Railway.

Body: 57′ 6″ × 9′ 3″
Seats: 1st, 16; **2nd,** 48
Weight: 26 tons 7 cwt

W56168 W56169

Swindon Works, B.R. (Inter-City) ■
Trailer Buffet First (L)

Introduced 1961.
Preserved at the North Yorkshire Moors Railway, Grosmont.

SC59098

Class 165 (4) ■
Metropolitan-Cammell
Trailer Buffet Second (L)

Introduced 1960.
Preserved by the Keighley & Worth Valley Railway Haworth.

Body: 57′ 0″ × 9′ 3″ Open second with miniature buffet at one end.
Weight: 25 tons
Seats: 2nd, 53

24 (E59575)

Metropolitan-Cammell

Pullman Motor Brake First (L)

Introduced 1959.
Preserved by the Blue Pullman Group.

Engines:
One North British/M.A.N. 12-cyl. pressure-charged V-type L12V18/21BS of 1,000 b.h.p.
Body: 66′ $5\frac{1}{2}$″ × 9′ 3″
Weight: 67 tons 10 cwt
Seats: 1st, 12
Transmission:
Electric. Two 425 h.p. G.E.C. traction motors driving through Brown-Boveri spring drive.

W60090 W60091

Swindon Works, B.R.

(Inter-City) ●

Trailer Buffet First (K)

Introduced 1957.
[1]Preserved at the Strathspey Railway, Boat of Garten.
[2]Preserved by the North Yorkshire Moors Railway, Grosmont.
Body: 64′ 6″ × 9′ 3″. Side corridor with seven first class compartments and end doors.
Weight: 33 tons 9 cwt
Seats: 1st, 42

SC79441[1] SC79443[2]

G.W.R. Railcars

Introduced 1934; *1940.
[1]Preserved at Didcot
[2]Preserved at the Kent & East Sussex Railway, Rolvenden.
[3]Preserved by the Great Western Society at Bridgnorth.

Engines:
Two A.E.C. 121 b.h.p.
*Two A.E.C. 105 b.h.p.
Seats: 2nd, 44; *48

W4W[1] *W20W[2] *W22W[3]

Waggon und Maschinenbau

Four-Wheel Railbus

Introduced 1958.
[1]Preserved by the Midland & Great Northern Preservation Society, Sheringham.
[2]Preserved at the Keighley & Worth Valley Railway, Haworth.

Engine:
Buessing 150 b.h.p. at 1,900 r.p.m.
*A.E.C. A220X type
Transmission:
Mechanical. Cardan shaft to ZF electro-magnetic six-speed gearbox
Body: 41′ 10″ × 8′ $8\frac{5}{16}$″
Non-gangwayed
Weight: 15 tons
Seats: 2nd, 56

E79960[1] *E79963[1] *M79964[2]
62(E79962)[2]

A.C.Cars

Four-Wheel Railbus

Introduced 1958.
[1]Preserved at the Somerset Railway Museum, Bleadon and Uphill station.
[2]Preserved by the North Yorkshire Moors Railway, Grosmont.

Engine:
B.U.T. (A.E.C.) 6-cyl horizontal type of 150 b.h.p.
Transmission:
Mechanical. Standard

Body: 36′ 0″×8′ 11″
Non-gangwayed
Weight: 11 tons
Seats: 2nd, 46

W79976[1] W79978[2]

Derby Works, B.R. (4)
Advanced Passenger Train

Introduced: 1972. Experimental four-car articulated unit, with a power car at each end
Preserved at the National Railway Museum, York
Engine:
Eight Leyland 350 automotive gas-turbines, rated at a nominal 298 h.p.
Transmission:
Four G.E.C. traction 253AY nose-suspended traction motors on the leading bogie only of each power car

APT–E

Electric Locomotives

Siemens Bo

Introduced 1898
Scheduled for preservation; at present in store at Preston Park.
System:
750 V d.c. 3rd rail

DS75

Brush Bo-Bo

Introduced 1904. One of two Class ES1 locomotives for shunting duties on the NER North Tyneside system.
Preserved at the National Railway Museum, York.
Equipment:
Four B.T.H. nose suspended traction motors
System:
630 V d.c. overhead and 3rd rail
Total h.p.: 640
Weight: 46 tons
Maximum tractive effort:
25,000 lb

26500

Battery Electric Bo

Introduced 1917. North Staffordshire Railway.
Preserved at the Staffordshire Industrial Museum, Shugborough Hall.
Equipment:
Two B.T.H. traction motors
Driving wheel diameter: 3′ 1″
Total h.p.: 82
Weight: 17 tons

BEL 2

British Railways Bo-Bo

Introduced 1950 for Manchester–Wath electrification.
To be preserved at York Museum.
Equipment:
Four 467 h.p. Metropolitan-Vickers nose suspended traction motors.
Driving wheel diameter: 4′ 2″
System: 1,500 V d.c. overhead
Total h.p. 1,868
Weight: 89 tons
Brake force: 43 tons
Maximum tractive effort:
45,000 lb.
Route availability: 8
Maximum speed: 65 m.p.h.

26020 (76020)

OTHER PRESERVED LOCOMOTIVES

Date built	Previous owner	Type	Locomotive	Place of preservation
1813	Wylam Colliery	0-4-0	*Wylam Dilly*	Scottish Museum Edinburgh
1814	Wylam Colliery	0-4-0	*Puffing Billy*	Science Museum, Kensington
1822	Hetton Colliery	0-4-0	No. 1	Beamish Museum
1825	Stockton & Darlington	0-4-0	*Locomotion*	Darlington, North Road Museum
1829	Liverpool & Manchester	0-2-2	*Rocket*	Science Museum, Kensington
1829	Bolton & Leigh	0-4-0	*Sanspariel*	Science Museum Kensington
1829	Shutt End Rly	0-4-0	*Agenoria*	Nat. Rly Museum
1830	Canterbury & Whitstable	0-4-0	*Invicta*	Canterbury Gardens
1830	Killingworth Colliery	0-4-0	*Billy*	Newcastle Museum
1837	GWR	2-2-2 Full-sized replica of the original	*North Star*	Swindon Museum
1838	Liverpool & Manchester	0-4-2	*Lion*	Liverpool Museum
1845	Grand Junction	2-2-2	No. 49 *Columbine*	Nat. Railway Museum
1845	Stockton & Darlington	0-6-0	No. 25 *Derwent*	Darlington North Road Museum
1846	Furness	0-4-0	No. 3 *Coppernob*	Nat. Railway Museum
1847	LNWR	2-2-2	No. 3020 *Cornwall*	BREL Crewe Works
1857	Wantage Tramway	0-4-0WT	No. 5 *Shannon*	Didcot
1865	LNWR	18" gauge	*Pet*	Narrow Gauge Museum, Towyn
1865	LNWR	0-4-0ST	No. 1439	Shugborough Hall
1866	MR	2-4-0 Class 1	No. 158A	Mid. Rly Trust
1866	Metropolitan	4-4-0T Class A	No. 23	Syon Park
1868	South Devon	Broad gauge 0-4-0T	*Tiny*	Newton Abbot Station
1869	NER	2-2-4T	No. 66 *Aerolite*	Nat. Railway Museum
1870	GNR	4-2-2	No. 1	Nat. Rly Museum
1872	Oxford & Aylesbury	0-4-0 Tram Locomotive	No. 807	Syon Park
1874	NER	0-6-0	No. 1275	Darlington Railway Museum
1875	NER	2-4-0 901 Class	No. 910	Nat. Railway Museum
1878	Gwendraeth Valleys	0-6-0ST	*Margaret*	Dyfed Museum, Haverfordwest
1882	LBSCR	0-4-2 Class B1	No. 214 *Gladstone*	Nat. Railway Museum
1885	Mersey Railway	0-6-4T	No. 5 *Cecil Raikes*	City of Liverpool Museum
1885	NER	2-4-0	No. 1463	Darlington Railway Museum
1887	LYR	18" gauge 0-4-0T	*Wren*	Nat. Railway Museum
1892	LNWR	2-4-0 Precedent Class	No. 790 *Hardwicke*	Nat. Railway Museum

Date built	Previous owner	Type	Locomotive	Place of preservation
1893	NER	4-4-0 Class M1	No. 1621	Nat. Railway Museum
1893	LSWR	4-4-0 Class T3	No. 563	Nat. Railway Museum
1893	Shrop. and Mont.	0-4-2WT	*Gazelle*	Nat. Railway Museum
1896	Metropolitan	0-4-4T	No. 1 (London Transport L44)	Quainton Road
1896	LYR	0-6-0ST	No. 752	K & WVR
1897	TVR	0-6-2T	No. 28	Caerphilly
1897	Alexandra Docks (GWR)	0-4-0ST	No. 1340 *Trojan*	Didcot
1898	GNR	4-4-2	No. 990 *Henry Oakley*	K & WVR
1899	TVR	0-6-2T	No. 52	K & WVR
1899	MR	4-2-2 115 Class	No. 673	Mid. Railway Trust
1900	Burry Port and Gwendraeth Valley	0-6-0ST	*Pontyberem*	Didcot
1902	GNR	4-4-2 Class C1	No. 251	Nat. Railway Museum
1906	GWR	0-4-0ST	No. 921	Leicester Corporation
1917	GSWR	0-6-0T	No. 9	Glasgow Transport Museum
1922	NSR	0-6-2T	No. 2	Shugborough Hall

Printed in Great Britain by Jarrold & Sons Ltd, Norwich

IAN ALLAN

IAN ALLAN TRANSPORT TRACKERS

Transport Trackers
have arrived!

If you are under 18 years of age and interested in transport, we want to help you increase your knowledge of the subject and have the opportunity of meeting others who share your enthusiasm. Already many young people are joining the TRACKERS and reaping the benefits of membership. All who join the IAN ALLAN TRANSPORT TRACKERS immediately receive a MEMBER'S FILE which includes:

- A MEMBER'S BADGE & CERTIFICATE
- CONCESSIONARY ENTRANCE/TRAVEL TICKETS TO MUSEUMS, RAILWAYS, AIR SHOWS, ETC.
- LIST OF ANNUAL EVENTS
- LIST OF PLACES OF INTEREST
- A 50p VOUCHER FOR IAN ALLAN PUBLICATIONS

Membership costs only 50p and, apart from the MEMBER'S FILE, many other special offers and privileges will be announced in the future.

I wish to join the IAN ALLAN TRANSPORT TRACKERS and enclose my membership fee of 50p incl VAT.

Name ....

Address ....

....

.... Age ....

Signature of parent/guardian ....

Special Interests ....

I enclose my cheque/postal order for 50p

Post to: TRANSPORT TRACKERS,
Terminal House · Shepperton · Middlesex TW17 8AS